THE SECULAR RELIGION OF FANDOM

SAGE SWIFTS

In 1976 SAGE published a series of short 'university papers', which led to the publication of the QASS series (or the 'little green books' as they became known to researchers). Almost 40 years since the release of the first 'little green book', SAGE is delighted to offer a new series of swift, short and topical pieces in the ever-growing digital environment.

SAGE *Swifts* offer authors a new channel for academic research with the freedom to deliver work outside the conventional length of journal articles. The series aims to give authors speedy access to academic audiences through digital first publication, space to explore ideas thoroughly, yet at a length which can be readily digested, and the quality stamp and reassurance of peer-review.

THE SECULAR RELIGION OF FANDOM

POP CULTURE PILGRIM

JENNIFER OTTER BICKERDIKE

 SAGE SWIFTS

 SAGE

Los Angeles | London | New Delhi
Singapore | Washington DC

Los Angeles | London | New Delhi
Singapore | Washington DC

SAGE Publications Ltd
1 Oliver's Yard
55 City Road
London EC1Y 1SP

SAGE Publications Inc.
2455 Teller Road
Thousand Oaks, California 91320

SAGE Publications India Pvt Ltd
B 1/I 1 Mohan Cooperative Industrial Area
Mathura Road
New Delhi 110 044

SAGE Publications Asia-Pacific Pte Ltd
3 Church Street
#10-04 Samsung Hub
Singapore 049483

Editor: Chris Rojek
Editorial assistant: Delayna Spencer
Production editor: Vanessa Harwood
Marketing manager: Michael Ainsley
Cover design: Jen Crisp
Typeset by: C&M Digitals (P) Ltd, Chennai, India
Printed and bound by CPI Group (UK) Ltd,
Croydon, CR0 4YY

Library of Congress Control Number: 2015950622

British Library Cataloguing in Publication data

A catalogue record for this book is available from
the British Library

MIX
Paper from
responsible sources
FSC
www.fsc.org   FSC® C013604

ISBN 978-1-4739-0779-9
eISBN 978-1-4739-1267-0

At SAGE we take sustainability seriously. Most of our products are printed in the UK using FSC papers and boards.
When we print overseas we ensure sustainable papers are used as measured by the Egmont grading system.
We undertake an annual audit to monitor our sustainability.

*To Mary McPherson - for being a truly uplifting,
open, beautiful, gracious, courageous soul.
Thank you for letting me be in your life.*

*To the mighty Chris Rojek - for being an
unerring source of inspiration, support, knowledge,
therapy, vino, friendship and overall amazingness.
I am forever in awe at my luck in knowing you.*

CONTENTS

ABOUT THE AUTHOR

Dr. Jennifer Otter Bickerdike is a Senior Lecturer in Music and Brand Management at Buckinghamshire New University. She has over 20 years of experience working with tastemakers and cultural provocateurs such as Facebook, Interscope Geffen A&M, Sony Music, Universal Music and Video Distribution, and L.A.M.B. She has helped create and implement marketing and promotion plans for some of the world's most iconic artists, including Sting, U2, Eminem, Dr. Dre, Gwen Stefani, Pearl Jam, Rage Against the Machine, and a little band called Nirvana. Jennifer's first book, *Fandom, Image and Authenticity: Joy Devotion and the Second Lives of Kurt Cobain and Ian Curtis*, was published in October 2014 by Palgrave Macmillan. Her work has been featured in several collections, including Mike Grimshaw's *The Counter-Narratives of Radical Theology and Popular Music* (2014, Palgrave Macmillan) and *Spirit of Talk Talk* (2012, Rocket 88). She was profiled in one of her lifetime heroine's books, Marlo Thomas's *It Aint Over Till It's Over* (2014, Atria Books), celebrating fearlessness and reinvention. She was also featured in a documentary on David Bowie for Ultimate Classic Rock, titled *30 Years of David Bowie's 'Let's Dance'*, and made her television debut in 2014 in the Channel 4 documentary *Frozen at Christmas*. She is currently editing a new book for Headpress on Joy Division fans, titled *Joy Devotion: The Importance of Ian Curtis and Fan Culture*. Her next project will be writing a book and producing a documentary movie on famous groupies from the late 1960s.

Other books by Jennifer Otter Bickerdike:

Joy Devotion: A Year of Trash, Trinkets and Tributes at the Ian Curtis Memorial Stone (2012, Blurb.com)

Fandom, Image and Authenticity: Joy Devotion and the Second Lives of Kurt Cobain and Ian Curtis (2014, Palgrave)

LIST OF FIGURES

ACKNOWLEDGMENTS

This would not have happened without my fabulous publisher, Chris Rojek, who has been an inspiration and supportive force throughout my entire life in the UK.

Thank you to all of my friends and family around the world who endlessly believe in me and make me feel like anything is possible. This book could not have happened without you. Special big hugs and kisses to Chris Baptie, Adrian Bossey, Alix Brodie-Wray, Gail Crowther, Niamh Downing, Leslie Dotson Van Every, Dan Heichel, Melissa Hidalgo, Krista Thorne-Yocam, Tom Ware, and the McPherson family. A special huge thank you to my family at the Oregon Music Hall of Fame (www.omhof.org) for changing my life so radically – Janeen Rundle, Inessa Anderson, Marc Baker, Bill Frith, Randy Hunzeker, J. Michael Kearsey, David Little, Geoff Metts, Wayne Pierce, Penny Williams, and especially my most worshipped and wonderful friend Terry Currier.

For the man I did not think existed – my wonderful, smart, and endlessly supportive husband James – I love you more than words can say.

INTRODUCTION: MECCA FOR MUGGLES

About a year ago, I was at King's Cross Rail Station in London. I am usually running late, completely focused on not missing whatever train or tube I am supposed to be on, so often utterly clueless on anything going on in my surroundings. This particular day, I was uncharacteristically early. I walked around, browsing the various shops and eateries that were on offer. At one end of the train station there was a huge snaking line. Curiosity got the better of me, and I got closer to have a better look as to what the attraction was.

It was a queue for Harry Potter. Harry Potter is, of course, the protagonist of the phenomenal series of books of the same name written by J.K. Rowling. The stories follow Harry as he leaves his English home to work on his inborn abilities of wizardry at Hogwarts, an exclusive school that teaches the necessary skills to succeed in the world of magic. Starring Daniel Radcliffe, movies based on the texts have spawned a global franchise, consisting of theme parks, toys, an entire online community dedicated to writing their own adventures of fan fiction using the Potter characters and a non-profit, the Harry Potter Alliance, whose mission is to 'turn fans into heroes' (The Harry Potter Alliance, 2005).

So what was the line for? No, not to meet Mr. Radcliffe or any of the other Hogwarts attendees who starred in the immensely popular films. The line was to have your picture taken next to the 'Platform 9 3/4' sign, fashioned to look like the very same spot where Harry starts his incredible adventure in both the books and the films. Though it was the middle of the week in the early afternoon – prime working hours – the line never dropped below 100 or so fans. This is not a surprising number, according to one of the guest services assistants, Harriet, who works at the site. Since opening on December 15, 2012, the platform hosts 'at least a thousand visitors day' (Harriet, 2015), with an increase during 'school holidays' (ibid.).

Once the devout reach the front of the queue, each person can pose with a Harry-esque luggage cart which looks to be hanging precariously between this world of 'muggles' (the term for the non-magically inclined used in the

Figure 1   Fans of Harry Potter pose at Platform 9 3/4 at King's Cross Rail Station, London, England. Photo: Jennifer Otter Bickerdike (2015)

Rowling books) and the land of wizards that Harry travels to to fulfill his destiny and learn about his powers. One employee of Platform 9 3/4 takes your picture, while another stands out of frame, to toss your scarf or pull your jacket, thus giving the same illusion in the photo of movement, of being pulled from one world to another as Harry was. Conveniently nestled right next door is the Platform 9 3/4 shop, where the avid can purchase an array of Potter items, from stuffed animals to sweaters, books to costumes.

The existence of Platform 9 3/4, and especially its tie-in retail shop, is a perfect example of modern-day, media-induced pilgrimage. The Platform exists solely both as an homage to the Potter books and as a way to draw customers to the shopping experience of the entire King's Cross complex, particularly the store dedicated to the space itself. It also clearly informs of a massive migration from fully fictional to existence and grounding in an actual place. I have been back to the area of King's Cross Station that houses Platform 9 3/4 several times since my initial encounter. On every occasion – no matter the season, the day of the week (though on weekends it is much busier, suggesting that tourists from the UK and EU as well as from far-flung locations are making their way to the attraction) – the queue remains at a solid minimum of 100 deep. The platform being the destination instead of just the mediating place of start or finish to a journey turns even the accepted and normative expectations and meaning for the location on its head, as this once transitional space becomes *the* place. By making something pretend actual, Platform 9 3/4 makes Potter actual, owning a space and place just as other working, 'real' platforms in the station. Perhaps, arguably, this 'pretend' shuttle between a real and an imaginary Potter world actually sees more people per day than some of the other active platforms within the station.

Platform 9 3/4 is just one of a myriad of possible examples illustrating how media pilgrimage has become a booming business in the 21st century. Fans of television, books, rock groups, and films flock to places associated with their favorite show, writer, artist, or movie, trying to embody and perhaps understand what inspired the beloved piece of work and, more importantly, to cobble together their own personal identity, seeking meaning in an ever more divergent and fast-paced world. At the same time, while technology allows for quicker connection on a global level than ever before, participation in organized group activities is dropping at an alarming rate. Robert D. Putnam (2001) refers to this as the 'Bowling Alone' phenomenon. His theory utilizes the recreational activity of bowling in the US as an example of decreasing social engagement in large, organized groups. There are less people bowling in leagues or formalized clubs; yet the raw number of people still participating in the sport has not declined. This acts as an illustration of the withdrawal from community, from group to individual; Putnam argues that this can be applied to explain the falling numbers in other real-time social activities, such as non-profit work, voter turnout, and committees.

CHURCH OF THE POISON MIND

One of the largest downturns in the US and the UK in such structured communal activities can be seen in the steep decline of attendance at many traditional Christian venues in the past decades.[1] In his 2014 article, 'Why Nobody Wants to Go to Church Anymore', Steve McSwain cites some staggering statistics highlighting the hemorrhaging of church goers in the US. He first addresses the Hartford Institute of Religion Research (no date) which recorded that 'more than 40% of Americans "say" they go to church weekly'. However, McSwain found that this rather robust figure is incorrect, as the same survey noted that 'less than 20% [of people who claimed to attend church weekly] are actually in church'. McSwain states, 'in other words, more than 80% of Americans are finding more fulfilling things to do on weekends'. The actual closure of physical spaces to follow traditional religious doctrine is shrinking as well in America. McSwain notes, 'somewhere between 4,000 and 7,000 churches close their doors every year', going on to quote Southern Baptist researcher Thom Rainer (2013) who 'puts the estimate higher … between 8,000 and 10,000 churches will likely close this year [in 2014]'. The trend it seems will continue, as few churches are seeing new affiliates as older ones die. McSwain underscores this, noting that 'between the years 2010 and 2012, more than half of all churches in America added not one new member. Each year, nearly 3 million more previous churchgoers enter the ranks of the "religiously unaffiliated"' (2014).

The UK has experienced a similar dramatic demise of participants, mirroring a move from traditional spaces and beliefs of religion toward a non-denominational, more personalized, secular identity. According to a new survey in 2014, 'In five decades, the number of people with no religion in Britain has grown from just 3 per cent of the population to nearly half … among adults aged under 25, nearly two-thirds define themselves as "nones", or people with no religious affiliation' (Gledhill, 2014). Gledhill argues that the fate of what has been considered traditional religion is in danger of becoming a thing of the past. Several strands of the Christian church, in particular, are in jeopardy of being fully eradicated within our lifetime if current behaviors move forward into the near future. Gledhill (2014) points out that, 'If the trends continue, Methodists

---

[1] While there has been growing numbers joining other religions such as Islam and sects such as evangelical Christianity, for the sake of this book, traditional, western, established practices of Christianity are the focus of the argument. A much different and just as relevant picture would surely emerge if the lens was placed on one of the other groups.

will be extinct in a few decades and the Church of England also faces massive decline by the end of the century'.

However, new groups inspired and based upon media and colonized via the internet are on the rise.[2] These virtual sites are often dedicated to pop culture and celebrities, as well as an ever more niche-focused array of real-time tours allowing fans to experience the spaces, places, and scenery featured in their favorite entertainment medium. This makes for a strong argument that media are replacing religion as the 'opiate for the masses' (Marx, 1843). Following the Marxist argument that 'Man makes religion, religion does not make man' (ibid.), man, therefore, creates technology and the beliefs and values it allows to be upheld and provoked. The revolution on every level of social interaction of the internet underscores the possibility of this hypothesis. In 2013, 83% of the British population had access to the World Wide Web, with 73% using the internet on a daily basis (Office for National Statistics, 2013). This is 20 million more users from the 2006 poll, the year when such statistics began being documented. In the US, almost 86% of the population are internet users, up by 7% in 2014 from 2013 (Internet Live Stats, 2014). On a global level, over '40% of the population has an internet connection today [March 15, 2015]. In 1995, it was less than 1%' (Internet Live Stats, 2015). Another survey looked across different online platforms to find a startling 11 hours spent by the average American adult per day on digital media (Petronzio, 2014). Britons are not far behind, allotting more time to the virtual universe than to one of the basic human necessities. Ofcom (Miller, 2014) found that 'UK adults spend an average of eight hours and 41 minutes a day on media devices, compared with the average night's sleep of eight hours and 21 minutes'. Looking specifically at social networking sites, Ofcom (2014) reported that 'Two-thirds (66%) of online adults say they have a current social networking site profile ... nearly all with a current profile (96%) have one on Facebook, three in ten social networkers say they have a Twitter profile, and one in five say they have a YouTube (22%) or WhatsApp profile (20%)'. Social networking overall remains a popular pastime, with 60% of users visiting sites more than once a day, an increase from 50% in 2012, and with 83% of those in the age group of 16–24 years doing so (69% in 2012) (Miller, 2014).

Ballve (2013) notes how Facebook still leads the pack of social media platforms, with over 1.15 billion monthly active users worldwide. The UK comes fifth in the world with over 30.3 million users of the site, with the US on top with over 151.8 million.

---

[2] Again, this is based on the accepted ideas of institutional Christianity.

All of these statistics illustrate how, metrically speaking, time spent on technology, digital media, and socializing in a virtual manner has not only replaced but arguably usurped old practices and beliefs, showing how popular culture could be moving from the profane to the sacred. Based upon sheer time and dedicated attention span, media have become the worshipped, proving a massive rupture in values and faith in the last half century from any time previous with the advent of an ever more variety of available frameworks to satisfy the seeming humanistic need to look for meaning outside of the individual. We have now emerged into an 'age of simulation ... [that] begins with a liquidation of all referential – worse: by their artificial resurrection in systems of signs' (Baudrillard, 1995: 4) – the sign, the image, the idea becoming fully authenticated without necessarily any substance to support it. This is perhaps not a new phenomenon; it is just the quicker evolution of popular belief systems aided by the instantaneous nature of the internet. As Baudrillard argues, 'All of Western faith and good faith was engaged in this wager on representation: that a sign could refer to the depth of meaning, that a sign could exchange for meaning and that something could guarantee this exchange' (1995: 10). He could be referring to an image of the Virgin Mary or the Facebook thumbs-up for 'liking' a post – they become interchangeable in the current literal 'marketplace' of faith where video game consoles, mobile phones, and Jesus are all competing for the time of a follower. As we look around for meaning, there is no 'real' truth, there is just the popular value system of any given time. What keeps a sense of religiosity afloat in any epoch is possibly the 'proliferation of myths of origins and signs of reality; of second-hand truth, objectivity and authenticity' (12). Within this context, religion and fandom can be synonymous, simply defined as a moveable feast of beliefs followed or adhered to by a defined group of people. However, some academics like Duffet do not agree to this theory. Duffet argues against the comparison of religion and fandom, which only succeeds in underscoring how similar they are. He contends, 'The "religiosity" idea maintains its grip by producing "evidence" that is an artifact of its own perception. Its central premise – that fandom is a religion because it looks like one – is weak because it is impossible to test conclusively in the field' (2003: 511). However, unlike a scientific test where there is usually a quantifiable answer, fandom and religion are both driven by faith, personal taste, and applicable societal norms differing for each individual. Duffet goes on to contradict himself, saying

> The question of whether the comparison [between religion and fandom] is valid appears to rest upon the precise desire of similarity: to say that fandom is a

religion is to assert that a line has been crossed. Yet fandom and religion are both abstract categories of collective experience. That line can never be clear and the question is impossible to answer conclusively with reference to field. (2003: 515)

Here he ascertains that as neither can be clearly defined, neither can, therefore, be discounted as not containing a subset of the other. Though he is arguing that fandom and religion are not the same, he simultaneously does not create a set of perimeters to either define each one or one from the other, therefore eliminating the possibility that fandom can act as religion. If viewed as substantive, religion clearly fits into the boundaries of fandom. Maybe one supports and defines the other, providing complimentary elements which alone one cannot grant. Thus fandom and religion may be neither the same nor different, but perhaps intertwined.

What about when religion fails? Even the most devout member of a faith must have moments of shaken validity of a benevolent God when confronted with the many atrocities of modern living. Where is this all mighty being when horrible things happen? The idea of religion catching and perhaps even protecting the individual from a fall seems inherently flawed when contrasted with the omnipresence of hardships. The object, however, is always available, with a similar array of believers to create community. For example, the music from a favorite artist or a movie featuring a comforting theme can appear to 'be there' when things go wrong, perhaps offering the solace not attained from traditional means of accepted worship. The internet, social networking, and other technological advances have dramatically increased the ease to connect with people who share such experiences, who may be obtaining such guidance and hope via a mediatized commodity not previously held in such high esteem.

The existence of Cullenists, a religion based upon the characters populating Stephenie Meyer vampire trilogy *Twilight*, underscores this seismic shift. Cullenists claim that they are '[j]ust like any other religion', that there is 'some spirituality to be had in the *Twilight* series, forming rules and principles upon which to base their tenets' (Bell, 2009). One of the base ideas of the faith claims that 'Edward and the rest of the *Twilight* characters are real', that '[t]he *Twilight* series should be worshipped' (ibid.). Cullenists are also expected to read from at least one of the vampire books a day in a Bible studyesque manner and make a pilgrimage to Forks, the town where the books/movies are set. The self-proclaimed 'rainiest town in the contiguous US' (Discover Forks Washington, 2015) makes the most of its inclusion in the best-selling novels. The Forks website invites visitors to 'explore the rain forest and beaches and just maybe, catch a glimpse of a vampire or werewolf!' in the same way that 'Bella [the female protagonist of *Twilight*] did' (ibid.). Forks has an annual event dually dedicated to *Twilight* writer Stephenie Meyer and to celebrate the birthday of fictional *Twilight* protagonist Bella. The Stephenie Meyer Day/ Bella's Birthday Weekend features a map of *Twilight*-specific spots to visit and the opportunity to sit in 'Bella's trucks' – automobiles resembling the ones used in the movies.

This book examines the function of such fandom, specifically the visiting of spaces like these which have been recently, through the media, deemed worthy of sanctification and a newly elevated status of importance. The book will look at how such pilgrimages are used as a means for forming and maintaining a common language of culture, creating a replacement apparatus based on more traditional frameworks of religious worship and salvation, while becoming an ever more dominant mechanism for constructing individuality and finding belonging in a commodified culture. What are the ramifications of placing such importance and mantle upon such media-driven vehicles – are they further separating us from authenticity and the very substance we long for? Or do they act as a means to form and connect to new communities in innovative ways?

Delving into these issues allows for a close scrutiny of spaces, fan communities, and rituals associated with each place, providing a unique and provocative investigation into how technology, media, and a humanistic need for guidance are forming novel ways of expressing value, forging self, and finding significance in an uncertain world.

IS FANDOM RELIGION?

In his book *Fans: The Mirror of Consumption*, Cornell Sandvoss (2005: 3) argues, it 'has become next to impossible to find realms of public life which are unaffected by fandom'. A quick glance around any grocery store, bus shelter, or Google search underscores his point, as the constant bombardment by pop culture to gain our attention and capture our money is omnipresent. Yet this alone does not religion make; it is the actions, beliefs, and meaning applied to the spaces and places associated with key entertainment entities which transforms the everyday to the hallowed, as the lens of devotion, previously often reserved for well-established saints and holy divinities, focuses on new destinations and icons.

Sandvoss and other academics acknowledge that there are various similarities between fandom and religion. Hills views that 'the correspondences between narratives of religious conversion and becoming a fan' as 'pat general-izations' (2002: 118). He perceives religion as providing the template or model for fan practice, as 'they are both centered around acts of devotion, which may create similarities of experience' (ibid.). Thus the language and behaviors of what he calls the 'discourse of religious conversion' bestows 'fans with a model for describing the experience of becoming a fan' (ibid.). Fandom, in this sce-nario, does not, therefore, replace religion; it just uses the cues and expected actions of religion as the framework for fan practices.

Sandvoss agrees that there is a big difference between religion and fandom as 'fans aim to take the place of the star in a way that is unlike religious devotion (in which devotees do not seek to supplant God)' (2005: 62). Hill and Jenkins (1992; cf. Hills and Jenkins 2002) also concede to 'the religious symbols and language in fandom containing analogies to religious doctrine', yet they view this as similar to 'other structures or institutions shaping and affirming identity, such as nation-states or ethnicity'. Sandvoss furthers this idea of identity, argu-ing that fandom is a form of self-reflection, as 'What qualifies fans' emphasis on the resemblance between themselves and their object of fandom … [is] not objectively verifiable, but based on the particular meaning which fans construct in their reading of the fan object' (2005: 103). He goes on to say that 'the object of fandom … is the coincidental medium of self-reflection, whose true quality lies in its reflective capacity', as 'the key indication of fans' self-reflective reading of their object of fandom then lies in the way in which they superim-pose attributes of the self, their beliefs and values systems and, ultimately, their sense of self on the object of fandom' (104). This once again brings back the interest not to the object of interest itself but to how that object relates and helps define the self.

There are two fundamental problems with these theories. First, Hill and Sandvoss both neglect to acknowledge that many religions and religious structures themselves are filled with the very 'pat generalizations' and 'self reflections' that they rail against. This is illustrated in the western world by the commonality of the 'salad bar' approach to religion – the taking on of those doctrines which an individual likes and/or feels applies to them and ignor-ing and/or not acknowledging the others. Even the religious portion of life has become viewed as a marketplace, where '"choice" has reigned supreme' (MacPhail, no date). A sermon from Reverend Bryn MacPhail illustrates this approach, 'We live in an society where choice has become one of our most esteemed freedoms' (ibid.). However, MacPhail bemoans the current state of many believers, arguing that individual choice does not have a place when interpreting the Bible and practicing faith. He states,

What I fear, however, is that many people import a salad bar mentality into their approach to the Christian life … [in a recent article [a] young churchgoer [was quoted] as saying, 'Instead of me fitting religion, I found a religion to fit me'. The writer of the article observed of this mentality, 'They don't convert – they choose' and 'by this standard, the most successful churches are those that most closely resemble a suburban shopping mall'. In the market place, choice is a good thing … At the salad bar we choose according to taste. We choose according to personal preference. At the salad bar, we load up on what we like, and we leave behind what we don't like. We cannot do the same as we approach the Bible. As we approach the Bible, we do not choose to believe the things we find palatable and leave the rest behind. (Ibid.)

MacPhail's points illustrate how the prevalent and long-established mechanisms of church-driven faith may be irrelevant in a customer world dominated by media and capitalism. One has to ask, if the rules laid out by the Bible, Koran, or any other spiritual text were all followed in exactly the same way, e.g. NOT in the very 'self-reflective' individualistic manner which Sandvoss attributes to fandom – would the different communities of the world be so at odds with one another? Arguably, religion itself is designed to be self-reflective. However, the manner by which it is often preached and practiced, as MacPhail's sermon astutes, is anything but not keeping pace with the current increasing importance placed on the individual. The metrics do not support conventional spirituality as a sustainable framework; on the contrary, church participation numbers dropping so dramatically has dovetailed with the massive uptick in social media, allowing formerly disconnected people around the globe to create increasingly niche-driven communities online. The internet in this manner becomes the conduit and incubator for endless varieties of fandom, with access to participate via the computer, tablet, or other handheld device as pervasive as prayer. Where the must-never-leave-home-without-it item was once a Crucifix or a set of rosary beads, the holy device du jour is now arguably the tablet, the mobile phone, or whatever portable technology is fresh from Silicon Valley. However, Sandvoss asserts that fandom

separates objective resemblance and self-reflection … [by] … the subjective reading position through which the fan finds his or her values and beliefs in the fan text. This self-reflective interpretation of the object of fandom discloses itself in the sheer range of varying, and frequently contradictory, readings of the same object of fandom by different fans and fan groups. (2005: 104–50)

His very ideas attempting to differentiate religion from fandom read as if he could be describing either one, as the lines in-between have become so blurred as to be indiscernible. Reverend MacPhail laments such picking and choosing of doctrines and scripture; however, the many perspectives and meanings of one of the original sources of textual worship, the Bible itself, provide support of the variable nuisances as prescribed by different groups of people. Maybe the followers of Jesus are an example of early fandom. Dyer's assertions of celebrity provide a lens through which to examine the validity of such a claim. He suggests,

> Like the sign, the celebrity represents something other than itself. The material reality of the celebrity sign – that is, the actual person who is at the core of the representation – disappears into a cultural formation of meaning. Celebrity signs represent personality – more specifically, personalities that are given heightened cultural significance with the social world. (2004: 56–66)

This together with the Sandvoss argument allows for the situating of the examination of fandom as religion. Yet as the Platform 9 3/4 example shows, what was once imaginary has now been subjugated by fandom to become real. As Baudrillard contends, 'the age of simulation thus begins with a liquidation of all referential – worse: by their artificial resurrection in systems of signs … substituting signs of the real for the real itself' (1995: 3–4). The virtual world allows for such interchangeability, for lines between frameworks to become obscured and even, in some cases, completely obsolete, as technology allows for more varied, more complex, and often more international structures to be built and nurtured in new and unprecedented manners, making formally assumed identities, i.e. nationalism or ethnicity, the supplementary form of individual identity. In these instances, belief and participation in fandom supersedes many other forms of previous worship, as 'It is now impossible to isolate the process of the real, or to prove the real' (Baudrillard, 1995: 41). For some, going to Platform 9 3/4 becomes as important than visiting Mecca; or perhaps Platform 9 3/4 is Mecca in this new economy where 'it is reality itself today that is hyperrealist' (147). The virtual and the real are often one and the same. It is the speed and capability of such technology that is the premium in how we connect – not necessarily real-time worship.

This shift can also be attributed to the role advertising and capitalism plays in the modern consumer's life. A 2007 study examining television habits of children under 18 found that the average child would view more than 20,000 individual advertisements in a year (Internet Resources to Accompany the Sourcebook for Teaching Science, no date), a figure that surely has ballooned since the increase in commercials becoming omnipresent on the internet. In his 2001 documentary *Merchants of Cool*, correspondent Douglas Rushkoff paints a much bleaker picture as to the sheer amount of advertising one has already encountered by age 18. He accepts that on any average day, a teenager in the US will view over three thousand discreet advertisements, and that by the time a young person is 18, they will have seen over 10 million discreet ads. There is endless opportunity for companies to try to 'convert' the young, as 75% of all teens have a TV in their own room, and one in three have their own personal computer on which they spend two hours on average a night (Rushkoff, 2001).

Many churches are even being encouraged to directly 'market' to possible attendees. This age group of digital natives – people who have grown up with the internet and web being a part of their daily lives – are 'adults aged under 25', a demographic where 'nearly two-thirds define themselves as "nones", or people with no religious affiliation' (Gledhill, 2014). Even religion itself is using the rhetoric of sales and marketing; as Gledhill admits, the findings present an enormous challenge for the churches over how they make faith appealing to young people, in a world where many young will be appalled at how the male-dominated church leadership has made discrimination against women and homosexuals a defining feature of orthodox mission.

Another issue is the 'failure to replace older generations of churchgoers' as the 'children of churchgoers are not attending as adults' (Gledhill, http://www.christiantoday.com, 2014). How to connect with young people? McSwain (2014) derides the current state of many churches as still operating in the age of the Industrial Revolution. Instead of embracing new means of communication and adapting their worship experiences to include technology, scores of traditional churches – mainly Protestant and almost all Catholic churches[3] – do not utilize the very instruments that most Millennials depend on to interpret their world. McSwain (2014) suggests,

> Pastors and priests … use social media and, even in worship … right smack in the middle of a sermon, ask the youth and young adults to text their questions about the sermon's topic … that you'll retrieve them on your smartphone … and, before dismissing, answer the three best questions about today's sermon.

His idea of trying to engage young people where they live – on the internet, via media devices – has often not been met with approval from many of his peers. McSwain reports, 'most of the ministers look at me as if I've lost my

---

[3] Though recently an iPad app called 'Confession: A Roman Catholic App' has been released, allowing even the most sinful to confess on-the-go.

mind' (ibid.), when he introduces such ideas. Rojek notes how important it is to recognize the changing modes of not only worship but how to communicate the message of the church itself:

> Religious belief is being reconfigured to provide meaning and solidarity as responses to the uprooting effect of globalization. Because these responses are communicated through the mass-media, they borrow the style and form of celebrity culture. (2001: 41)

With such resistance to speak to young people in a way which matches up with the current expected mechanisms for dialogue in the 2.0 world, it is not surprising to see such a drop in participation of customary worship. McSwain (2014) points out that instead of worrying about possible unorthodox manners of preaching the gospel, today's religious leaders should be more concerned about 'why the Millennials have little or no interest in what they [religious leaders] have to say'.

This further shows how the instant accessibility on a global level has made the populace equally more connected and further isolated, as we move from formerly group activities to lone participation – attending a church service and sharing a communal experience with others shifts to a text message solely for the individual on the personal handheld device. Instead of watching a movie with several hundred others at a large cinema, the film moves to the family home to be viewed by only those in the room, to the individual looking at a smartphone or a tablet in a lone hand, headphones plugged in, a score heard only by the sole listener. In one way, it is a shift to belief in a virtual place without a space; on the other hand, it releases one from former accepted manners for anchoring significance through a shared experience and authenticity as prescribed by assumed meanings.

Hill, Sandvoss, and other academics of their ilk preach that fandom and religion are black and white, that they are not the same, and though some of the behaviors associated with fandom may resemble acts traditionally attributed to formulated theological practice, the two are different. However, those at the sharp end in the field, such as McSwain, MacPhail, and Gledhill, illustrate the actual reality of the state of religion in the western world currently. For many, it is a pick-and-mix to reflect one's own personal belief system, not an indoctrinated and blindly accepted code of beliefs as often preached. This makes for very grey religion; what is religion, and what is worship in this technology-ruled, consumer-driven marketplace where even faith is grappling for the attention of possible buyers, er, converts? Sandvoss's claim that the fan wants to embody and become the idol again seems to be describing not necessarily contemporary and normalized fandom but the very sacraments of the Christian church, where the confirmed drink wine to represent and embody the blood of Christ, the bread wafer consumed in place of the body of the divine son of God. Rojek goes further with this connection, stating,

> Other than religion, celebrity culture is the only cluster of human relationships in which mutual passion typically operates without physical interaction. The general form of interaction between fan and the celebrity takes the form of consumer absorbing a mediated image … Religion … refers to the formulation of belief in a general order of existence, in which powerful, durable attachments are invested in spiritually relevant objects or persons. (2001: 48–9)

Arguably these holy acts of worship inside the church are the clearest examples of wanting to become the very entity of worship, the 'durable attachments', as taking the communion puts Christ directly into the body of the believer, thus taking a piece of their idol and having it become part of the devout. Sandvoss's focus on the fans – not on the accepted practices of many Christian churches – of imbibing their God once again only underscores the ever more interchangeable nature between the frameworks and practices of religion and fandom. It could be argued using Sandvoss's very theory that the church attendees are simply huge fans of Jesus – which removed from the accepted narrative of religion and the historical context of baggage associated with it, surely they could be. Rojek sees, 'in the absence of a unifying deity, some people search for cult figures to give life new meaning' (2001: 95). He views 'celebrity culture [not as] a substitute for religion' (97). Instead, he sees religion as providing the frameworks for how we relate to celebrity and act as fans. His ideas lend themselves to support the idea that what has traditionally been viewed as the all-seeing hand of the church is really outdated, arguing

> Today perhaps only family rivals celebrity culture in providing the scripts, prompts and supporting equipment of 'impression management' for the presentation of self in public life. Indeed, a good deal of evidence, notably the high rate of divorce and the rising number of single-person households, suggests that the family is in decline, while celebrity culture seems to be triumphant ascendant. (Ibid.)

Celebrity, and the media used to create, sustain, and continue interest in fan communities, has more importance in the daily lives of the average westerner than ever before. As we leave the conventional idioms of holiness behind in our dot-com world, there is still a need to look to something, someone for guidance. Many people are at least vaguely familiar with the basic frameworks of religion. This makes a perfect atmosphere for celebrity and fandom to act as a modern arena of reverence, based on images and ideas already known and accepted by many, allowing for an individualized belief system populated by bespoke icons taken from a variety of reference points. According to Rojek, 'fans today ... seek out celebrities to anchor or support [the fans'] personal life' (2001: 74). Celebrity culture is custom-fit for this use, having an endless array of individuals, places, and interests propelled via the media as having assumed importance. As Rojek points out, 'Celebrity culture is secular. Because the roots of secular society lie in Christianity, many of the symbols of success and failure in celebrity draw on myths and rites of religious ascent and descent' (74). Fandom thus enters a new epoch, one where it is not only the language, actions, and modes but the normalized participation of such ritual which can come to replace past religious roles. Instead of the martyred glorified soul, it is the 'celebrities [who] provide us with heroic role models in an age of mass standardization and predictability' (93).

I'LL BE YOUR SAINT

In his 2002 book, Hills makes the distinction between a celebrity and an icon. A celebrity, he suggests, in the tradition of Daniel Boorstin (1962), is 'often considered to be a synthetic creation, made for the purposes of audience appeal and subject to the transient and fleeting touch of "fame"'. The icon, on the other hand, 'moves continuously across social historical frames, being re-mapped and reworked in this process: it's iteration, or an accreting set of iterations' (Hills, 2002: 140). However, Hills argues, neither 'stars [nor] celebrities ... are ... mythical heroes' (142–3). This is problematic, as often repeated tales of triumph over adversity to reach astronomical heights (see Elvis Presley, Eminem, Oprah Winfrey) have become the backbone to the western world's narrative of self-made wo/man. Marshall underscores this point, as 'The star is meant to epitomize the potential of everyone in American society' (1997: 9) – the myth of the availability of high financial achievement being a unilaterally reachable goal to aim for. Dyer echoes this sentiment, as 'the star is universally individualized, for the star is the representation of the potential of the individual' (2004: 16). He also again asserts a parallel between celebrities and gods, as an apparatus to order and make sense of life. He states,

> Stars represent typical ways of behaving, feeling and thinking in contemporary society, ways that have been socially, culturally, historically constructed ... Stars are also embodiments of the social categories in which people are placed and through which they have to make sense of their lives, and indeed through which we make our lives categories of class, gender, ethnicity, sexual orientation and so on. (Ibid.)

Just as the lessons learned from saints or other religious figures have provided a sense of order, now the stories of the stars, especially those who died young and tragically,[4] provide the template for how we should be living our lives. They become immortal, as in our secular society the honorific status conferred on certain celebrities outlasts physical death (Rojek, 2001: 78). Their lives – or, more accurately, the way their lives are portrayed through the media – position them as 'the heroes of popular culture [that] simultaneously offer hope for everyone's success and the promise of the entire social system to be open to these moments of luck' (Dyer, 2004: 9). Rojek supports this idea of the 'new' legends of the celebrity as the modern-day folk stories, pointing out that 'The wealth, freedom and popularity of stars fulfilled the American dream. Hollywood celebrities were self-made individuals who achieved their wealth and power by their talents and industry'. He more fully fleshes out the mystical aura surrounding the famous, stating 'celebrities often seem magical or superhuman' (2001: 13). He also makes the connection between traditional idols found in conventional forms of worship and celebrity culture, arguing that 'celebrities replaced the monarchy as the new symbols of recognition and belonging, and as the belief in God waned, celebrities became immortal' (14).

MEDIA PILGRIMAGE AND THE DARK TOURIST

I'm going to Graceland

Graceland

In Memphis Tennessee

I'm going to Graceland

Poorboys and Pilgrims with families

And we are going to Graceland

My traveling companion is nine years old

---

[4]   Therefore they cannot be making outlandish and loutish commentary on social media, putting out an unpopular piece of work or committing the biggest sin of aging.

He is the child of my first marriage

But I've reason to believe

We both will be received

In Graceland ...

[...]

But I've reason to believe

We all will be received

In Graceland

('Graceland', Paul Simon, *Graceland*, Warner Brothers, 1986)

From his 1986 Grammy award-winning album, Simon places the former home and final resting place of Elvis Presley as worthy of reverence and a place of comfort, likening the Memphis Tennessee destination to a holy ground. The wording he chooses echoes the phraseology which one would expect to accompany the description of a church or other sacred institution where the downtrodden – those looking for sanctuary and divinity – can find relief and look to bring reinvigoration to spiritual beliefs. The 'poorboys and pilgrims with families' as well as Simon's own 'child of [his] first marriage' make for a divergent description of the vulnerable, destitute, and those living with the broken bonds of holy matrimony (as divorce is often viewed by the Catholic church as a major sin against God), all going to see the space made famous by the King. Yet Simon's carefully picked words – 'we both will be received', in fact, 'we *all* (my emphasis) will be received/In Graceland' – speak to both the inclusive nature of such spaces as well as the power of the mediated myth of Elvis – the country boy born in a two-room home in Tupelo, Mississippi, going on to be one of the most significant cultural figures in the 20th century and beyond.

These feelings are not unique to the travelers in Simon's song, as, according to Rojek, 'the pilgrims who flock to Graceland, the burial place and former home of Elvis Presley, do not so much honor a dead God as proclaim the presence of a living secular one in popular culture' (2001: 63). Going to a place linked to such a figure allows the fan/pilgrim to feel closer through proximity. This is often crucial for maintaining and rooting continued investment in the idol, as 'relationships between fans and celebrities frequently involve unusually high levels of non-reciprocal emotional dependence, in which fans project intensely positive feeling onto the celebrity' (51).

Elvis makes for an interesting case study for the specific cross-roads of death and media creating the perfect storm of rebirth – the emergence of a perfect icon, rising from the death of a conflicted, complicated human. The dead cannot speak for themselves, allowing any assortment of ideas, values, and mythology to be projected onto them. Any physical objects left behind – images, music, movies, even personal belongings – shift from a mere material good to a sacred item, entrenched with deeper and more important relevance than existed before death. The importance to fans of visiting the space once occupied by Elvis provides another parallel between fandom and religion, as 'the preservation of relics from the bodies and possessions of the saints is a common feature of religious practice' (Rojek, 2001: 59). Even the most mundane of object – a scrap of hair, a discarded school card – is transformed from the everyday to the sacred. Death allows for the retelling of the icon's story and the ability for him/her to be reframed as an aspirational, flawless good ad infinitum, as 'death provides no obstacle to the commodification of the celebrity' (60).

Hills uses Presley to summarize this post-mortem phenomenon, stating, 'death cleansed Elvis – even the scandalous type of death which claimed him – replacing the grotesque narrative of an excessive and, in many ways, foolish life, with an absolutely irrational and enigmatic end-point' (2002: 141). He goes on to point out that through distribution and replication, Elvis changes, evolves, blurs from a troubled human to that of an easy-to-understand and quick process: 'Elvis becomes a cult icon by virtue of his image's persistence and his reproduction or reiteration across generations and across social-historical contexts' (141–2). Yet it is not the 'real' Elvis that is being adored – but this new version, the good-looking, safe model – with all the rough corners, deep-fried-sandwich loving, drug snarkeling, womanizing ways cut off and left out.

Graceland provides a physical grounding place for the Presley legend. This makes his 'story' appear to be based in a reality instead of simply an ethereal narrative. Visitors will all be received at the mansion, as long as they can cough up the variable ticket price of $36–77 (£24–52) for entry. Hills contends,

> While Graceland certainly didn't make Elvis into a star … the house has had a significant and largely unacknowledged – impact on the shape of Elvis's stardom ever since he purchased it in March 1957. Graceland gave Elvis something no other US celebrity of the twentieth century had: a permanent place to call 'home' that was as well known as its celebrity resident. (2002: 154)

Rodman echoes the importance of real-time space in the King's lasting appeal, 'Perhaps the single most important effect that Graceland had on Elvis's public image is that it gave his stardom a stable, highly visible, physical anchor in the real world' (1996: 99). More importantly, it provided Elvis's fans – and the mythos of Elvis – a place to go to, the opportunity to literally retread the footsteps of their fallen idol. Instead of Elvis mania being an untouchable firmament, the stories now had tangible materiality.

Such a mix of death and travel can be defined as a form of dark tourism, a purposeful visit for leisure to places where a macabre, grisly event, or tragedy occurred – usually something so horrific, it pushes the mind to reenvision how it could have actually happened. Rojek suggests that such spaces are 'black spots', specific locations – like the Memphis mansion – marked by the death of a famous person (1993: 137–45). Going to such places is a growing industry, as 'tourist interest in recent death, disaster and atrocity is a growing phenomenon in the late twentieth and early twenty-first centuries' (Foley & Lennon, 2010: 3). Though the media have glorified the burgeoning business of such trips – after all, 'death has become a commodity for consumption in a global communications market' (5) – it is most likely not a new occurrence. Foley and Lennon concede,

> Several commentators view pilgrimages as one of the earliest forms of tourism; this pilgrimage is often (but not only) associated with the death of individuals or groups, mainly in circumstances which are associated with the violent or untimely. Equally, these deaths tend to have a religious or ideological significance, which transcends the event itself to provide meaning to a group of people. (3)

The story of the death, and the places associated with the figure, often becomes more important than any legacy they may have created during their lives, as '[the death itself] spawn[s] fascination and public ownership of death which has almost eclipsed their [the icons] lives. This kind of fascination appears to be an aspect of commodification of these individuals as icons via the media' (Foley & Lennon, 2010: 168). As they become a product with an attached consumer as well as cultural value, these very places, spaces, and ideas which made them famous in the first place are often leeched of their power through a seeming collective forgetfulness of the more troubling aspects of life, as 'there is an inherent danger in constant re-creation of the past, particularly if there is any attempt at stylization which can marginalize and indeed trivialize the enormity of the issues being dealt with' (29). Graceland is a shining example of this. The kitchen of the mansion where Elvis's artery-clogging, deep-fried pickles were prepared now transforms into a place where his holiness took his daily (deep-fried) bread. The upstairs of Graceland – where Presley's bed and bathroom are located – are off limits to any public viewing, thus literally editing and curating not only the shrine of Graceland itself but the story of who and what Elvis was from the accessible glimpse. Dying in the toilet from an overdose of prescription drugs does not a romantic (and profitable) myth make – thus the last rooms actually inhabited by a living Presley are completely erased from the story itself as well as made invisible to the pilgrims' eye. Even the means by which the rags-to-riches tale is told to guests of the mansion – via personal handheld sets, 'audio guided tour[s]' (Graceland, 2014), in 9 different languages[5] – is narrated by a D-list actor, Elvis wanna be John Stamos, best known for his character of rebel-musician (sound familiar?) Uncle Jesse on US cheese-fest sitcom *Full House*.

Graceland is the epitome of a re-envisioned past come to life, offering a template for other makeovers of rock-and-roll legend, as 'the interpretation and re-telling of events surrounding the death have shaped perceptions of reality, in projecting visitors into the past; reality has been replaced with omnipresent simulations and commodifications' (Foley & Lennon, 2010: 79). No matter how grisly such spaces may be when pulled apart and closely examined, they provide the cross-cultural, omni-societal means for communication; they 'have become international markers of collective memory' (ibid.).

Hills solidifies the link between religion and secular pilgrimage with the example of Graceland. He suggests, like Rodman, that the mansion provides a concrete place for Elvis's fans in a similar way that churches act to congregate believers.

> Through Graceland, the significance of Elvis – something which would otherwise tend to be free-floating, and incidental to processes of signification – can be contained or 'anchored' in a visible, physical and public fashion ... it provides a form of permanence to what would otherwise be a potentially fleeting pre-verbal experience. Hence the repeated importance of physical spaces and architecture within all forms of organized religion. Sacred spaces do not simply reproduce sacred/profane oppositions, neither are they merely 'containers' for the purity of the sacred, as these forms of behavioral legislation emerge after the fact. The 'church' is first and foremost a physical anchor for the 'oceanic feelings' of the devout; it serves to 'hold' the original emotional experience which prompts a sense of sacredness. (2002: 154)

---

[5] English, German, Italian, Dutch, Portuguese, Spanish, Japanese, Mandarin Chinese, and French.

In this manner, Graceland is the church, the graves of the Presley family making it a sacred, consecrated space. The house itself comes to be the physical container for the attachments and beliefs bestowed to the King. Having such a permanent spatial marker allows for the values attributed to Presley to be both free-flowing through an individual's own personal belief system as well as simultaneously having a literal home encasing all of the 'relics' and legends of the rock star. The ability to be able to walk the same stairs that HE walked and to view the same pictures hanging on the walls of the mansion that Elvis himself once took in creates an ethereal bond between devotee and icon, crossing time, place, gender, and social economic standing. As Sandvoss writes of the mansion, 'the emotional significance of visiting fan places lies in the ability of fans to put themselves physically in the otherwise textual universe' (2005: 61). The help of the internet and the World Wide Web aides this even further – the Graceland Live Cam allows visitors from anywhere to see what is happening at any given time at the King's home (from two different perspectives, the side of the house and a full frontal shot). Updated every 60 seconds, the Live Cam further bestows a sense of importance on the myth of Presley and the place the Graceland mansion plays in his omnipresence in current modernity. The minute-to-minute updates create a sense of immediacy, as if something of incredible gravity is about to happen,[6] the cameras allowing no one, no matter where placed on the globe, to be left behind from its impact.

Within this context, travel becomes dual – a limitless, untethered internet community, which is often fueled and perpetuated by the action of visits to real-time space. This makes the various forms of media tourism – from the bus loads of *Sound of Music* fans in Salzburg, gaping at the hills where Julie Andrews twirled about the sloping greenery in the iconic 1965 film, to those visiting sites associated with much more macabre pasts in various forms of dark tourism, namely the graves of dead rock stars – sacred pilgrimages to holy grounds which fuel entire belief systems, social groups, and salvation.

MEDIA, MESSIAHS, AND MATERIALITY

Using these frameworks, each chapter will look at a different aspect of media which has spurred an ever-growing industry of pilgrimage to a variety of places. This allows for a closer examination of how each space, place, and form of engagement leads every place to have special, sometimes even sacred meaning

---

[6] I have logged on to the site dozens of times and have never seen anything happening – not even people walking around. It is just a stagnant picture of a house, caught by rather dodgy security cameras.

to those visiting it (while still remaining lacking of any note for those not in the 'know'). Looking at the transition from mundane to iconic bestowed-upon specific locations as well as to defined individuals will allow for a more robust understanding of the intersection between media, the making of modern messiahs (fictional, mythical, and a combination of both), as well as how materiality of place creates new meaning for a divergent assortment of formerly indistinguishable sites.

The first chapter will examine how popular television series have transformed specific locations related to fictional shows to destinations for enthusiasts. This creates a melding of real and imagined, fictional and idealized, constructing a lived experience from one which has only been showcased through a fantastical story. *The Walking Dead* has captured the largest and most-sought-after chunk of the 18–45- year-old market. As the zombie rages on the small screen, fans of the television show flock to the cobbled tour, taking visitors around Atlanta and through some of the areas included in the five seasons of the series. Trying to capitalize on the cult hit *Game of Thrones*, several companies now offer tours in Ireland and Iceland, taking pilgrims to key spots seen in pivotal scenes. British hit show *Doc Martin* uses the Cornish seaside village of Port Isaac – renamed 'Portwenn'[7] for the show – as the setting for its quirky, gentle comedy-drama. Though extremely different in their locations, cultural heritage, and context, each of the places has been literally reimagined through television, the behavior of visitors to these spaces, and the melding of a created, invented world with real-time consequences.

The second chapter will delve into the rituals, beliefs, and meaning applied to specific locations associated with legendary music icons and how such performance affects memory, commodity, and secular worship. Sonic pilgrimage has become a normative part of the participatory culture of rock music, perpetuating the importance and exalted status of key artists in a search for personal identity. Such trips also aide in creating a shared context for cultural belonging within a larger fan community. Key spots associated with some of Manchester, England's, most beloved bands – The Smiths, Joy Division, The Stone Roses – and iconic entities – Tony Wilson, Factory Records, the Haçienda – will allow for an in-depth look at how and why these places have become endowed with greater significance through the power of song.

Moving down to Barnes, a sleepy, upper crust borough located in outer London, the Marc Bolan Rock Shrine holds place of prominence and contrast

---

[7]   Some places have it spelled 'Port Wenn', and others as one word, 'Portwenn'. For our purposes, the fictional village will appear from here as 'Portwenn'.

in a very affluent community. Erected on the spot where his car fatally hit a sycamore tree in 1977, the Shrine has received various accolades, including being recognized in 1999 by the English Tourist Board's publication of England Rocks! as one of the 113 'Sites of Rock "N" Roll Importance' in England. However, its placement – right in the middle of a neighborhood where studio apartments start at a cool £1 million – begs the question of its importance and staying power for the longer term; as each passing year ticks by since Bolan's death, the property prices get ever higher, and perhaps a feather boa, beer bottle-adorned tree, and glittery accoutrements may not be viewed as the best use of highly valuable real estate – not to mention what neighbors want to see when returning to their pricey abodes.

Comparing the tiny, under reported, 'do-it-yourself' character of the Bolan Shrine with spaces in the north – made famous through movies such as *24 Hour Party People, Control,* and *Live Forever* – provides the opportunity to examine fan behaviors, motivations, and beliefs at two radically different places centered on divergent figures. This gives insight into how technology, specifically social media platforms, allows for continued cultural investment and expanding importance placed upon such pop heroes within the context of both real and virtual space.

Chapter 3 will examine the tradition of literary tourism and how it has come to play an important role in maintaining an author's toe-hold in the current marketplace. It will also look at how modern mania has made holy shroud from even the most humble of accoutrements previously owned by famed writers and how this value evolves, mutates, and possibly distorts the original work itself. Using a variety of locations – the settings for Bram Stoker's legendary *Dracula,* the ties between Daphne du Maurier and Cornwall, Haworth and the Brontës – this chapter delves into the importance of space, real and imagined, for creating identity from the pages of a book.

The act of pilgrimage is not new; however, the variety of places on offer and deemed worthy of such behavior has grown exponentially over the last twenty years, as the internet has allowed for ever more divergent groups of communities to form and prosper through global engagement. This book sets out to support the thesis that secular pilgrimage to places of pop culture importance may be a new form of religion, as our ever more mediated world tells us that it is celebrity, technology, and often fame which is valued above all else.

I

SYMBOLIC PILGRIMAGE

Using the word 'action' to describe sitting down to veg out in front of a TV seems like an oxymoron. The act of watching TV is most often associated with tuning out the 'real world' and becoming one with the sofa – hence the popular 'couch potato' tag long used for individuals who lay slug-like in front of the boob tube for hours on end. The parasocial relationships that are formed, however, between the viewer and the characters populating a television series can be very profound. These are individuals who are coming into the home on a regular basis – daily, in the case of soap operas like *Coronation Street* – or weekly, with *The Walking Dead*. This is not to mention the ability via streaming services to literally have a favorite show with one at all times, as on-demand services allow for whenever, wherever watching. With such exposure available, an individual may have more interaction with a fictional protagonist from the small screen – coming into the house/handheld personal space on a regular, often weekly basis – than with a loved one.

Perhaps putting on a favorite show can be a form of pilgrimage, of escaping the daily grind to a different reality. Professor Will Brooker argues that maybe this seemingly passive, often dismissed form of entertainment holds far greater meaning in our spiritual life than previously thought. He realizes that 'the idea that watching television constitutes a "symbolic pilgrimage" may still prompt a skeptical response' (2007: 149), yet still asks if 'instead of treating symbolic pilgrimage as a separate category, we should ask whether all geographical pilgrimage in fact involves a degree of conceptual, inner, symbolic travel' (150). While this may sound initially like a bit of a stretch, Brooker points out that such metaphorical, metaphysical journeys have long-reaching roots, as 'this notion of passage as a spiritual and symbolic state rather than a literary movement can be identified in Christianity, as well as African tribal culture' (151–2). Like the practices of other recognized religions, Brooker notes 'how some form of preparation ritual is not uncommon among media fans ... this often seems to approach an act of communion, a symbolic activity that removes the participant from the everyday and brings him or her closer to the fiction' (155). In his previous work on fans, Brooker found that respondents found viewing of a favorite television show 'a transition to a world "between the real and unreal"' (1999: 165), 'a sacred place where "real" time and space are excluded' (164). Brooker's analysis also showed that 'the community is also symbolic, and can take place even if the individual is sitting alone, as "despite watching the show by themselves, they feel attached to the community of non-present viewers"' (168). This surely is even further buttressed by real-time interactions offered on such platforms as Facebook and Twitter, where commentary evolves before, during, and after the television show has been aired. When Brooker published his findings in 1999, he noted that, 'This congregation, an invisible network uniting fellow fans independent in part on traditional schedule-based broadcasting, so the viewer can imagine millions of others doing the same thing at the same time – unites individual viewers ... in a kind of intellectual elite' (Brooker, 2007: 158). Here Brooker references the assumed perimeters and language of religious groups, a 'congregation'; yet the church in this instance is the television, the pews the individuals' sofa from where they watch the show. Such phenomenon has surely only grown with the explosion of apps, websites, and the instant availability of information and opinion in the coinciding years.

The virtual communities of television predated online networks, yet within the current economy, the latter helps to create new bonds and evoke deeper meaning for the former. By 'experiencing' the same thing with others around the world, a new definition and form of participation is forged, where boundaries of spatial consequence are broken down, or perhaps even non-issues. Here fans from across the world can share a pilgrimage to the same place at the same time which may have the same profound meaning to their lives as a visit to the actual place. Brooker believes that "symbolic pilgrimage" is more than just a subcategory of or poor cousin to "real" geographical journeys, offering a fainter taste of the same sensations and a shallower sense of connection. In fact, symbolic immersion and psychological leaps of faith are integral to many, perhaps the majority, of geographical media pilgrimages (Brooker, 2007: 163).

The fan must, therefore, first journey symbolically, e.g. without physically going to a specific place to understand its meaning, and have the ability to decode the significance of certain sites and spots associated with the focal text. The symbolic pilgrimage allows for the richest understanding and experience with the site of a text and a space of secular worth as mediated by the television show community's beliefs and values.

Sylvia Plath scholar Gail Crowther further underscores this point, the importance of knowledge acquired through symbolic pilgrimage. In her own travels to retrace the steps of the famous poet, Crowther relates how she has already 'been' to many of the places tied to or associated with Plath's short life. Crowther writes,

> I have never been to America, my neighboring country across the Atlantic from here in England, yet I really have walked the streets of Boston. For Boston exists in a virtual space, its buildings and roads there to be walked and strolled with one click of a button on Google Street View. (2010: 1)

As she encounters various landscapes Plath wrote about through her internet connection, Crowther notes, 'I am simultaneously responding to the traces someone left fifty two years ago right there, yet mediated through the screen of my computer' (2010: 2).

As we become more digitally and technology indebted, it is becoming harder and harder to differentiate between such 'real' and 'ethereal' space. Crowther uses theory from Mark Nunes to further support this dual importance of both the seemingly 'actual' (the physical) and the 'virtual' (online) place. 'Nunes argues that virtual space is not really non-corporeal or simply a mental space because in order for it to be produced, it requires the presence of laptops, computer terminals and the cramped fingers of the corporeal body working the keyboard' (Crowther, 2010: 3–4; Nunes, 2001). This makes the 'virtual' perhaps on par with the 'real', if not at least a springboard for increasing interest in visiting the actual and informing the feelings, beliefs, and practices at specific sites.

When approaching the three television case studies examined here – The Walking Dead, Game of Thrones, and Doc Martin – it begs to question what these divergent places and series have in common. The trait they all share is the way that secular pilgrimage has dramatically changed the communities to where such travels occur. In all three case studies, the uptick in newly founded importance to each place associated with the television shows has contributed to the economic benefit and survival of the spaces. This makes the native stakeholders just as beholden to upholding and perhaps perpetuating the value of each of these areas, providing another layer of investment and meaning.

While the locals in these disparate examples all appear to have had their fortunes changed by such en masse tourism, the reasons for the trips themselves and the ideals motivating each pilgrimage differ greatly. The Walking Dead offers an imagined landscape of post-apocalyptic diaspora, a reinvention of the human condition. *Game of Thrones* has a similar fantastical appeal, being set in world resembling but not completely our own. However, pilgrims to the setting of this show are looking to convene not with a seemingly alternative version of reality offered by *The Walking Dead*; instead, they want to be immersed in a fictional world much different to the one they know in all but the most perfunctory of ways. The landscape of *Game of Thrones* is the closest opportunity to interact with the show in a three-dimensional, palpable manner. *The Walking Dead* is also a created universe, a nightmare vision of modern humanity. Yet the difference between pilgrims to *The Walking Dead* and *Game of Thrones* locations is the former are attempting to recapture or perhaps further make sense of the bleakest future of humanity, while the latter are looking to pin the fantastical to the real; thus the need to shore up the 'virtual' and 'real' with the imagined and physical is blurred in both visits. While the needs of the pilgrim to somehow get closer and further bestow the text of the shows with meaning are similar, the deeper motivations and values offered by the two spaces are opposite. *The Walking Dead* is a fantasy of worse-case scenario, while *Game of Thrones* is a parallel universe entirely.

In contrast, *Doc Martin* fans visiting Port Isaac are seeking to experience the seemingly gentler, simpler life as portrayed on offer in the light-hearted British show. *Doc Martin* seems real – the characters populating the scenes of each episode could be actual people. Indeed, some of the cast of the show are made up of natives and locals, blurring the lines between material and scripted. While *The Walking Dead* and *Game of Thrones* visitors are looking to ground the fictional in the corporeal, *Doc Martin's* small Cornish village looks and feels as if you could truly step into the show. Trips to Port Isaac further this allusion, as the sites, smells, and people are almost identical to the ones viewed on television, thus making the visitor feel as if they have already been to the town.

They arguably have – through countless evenings engaging on 'symbolic' pilgrimages mediated at home. Stijn Reijnders examined the motivation of media pilgrims, using *Dracula* tourism as his primary subject group. After substantial field work, Reijnders found that the desire to visit actual places where fictional works were set fell primarily into

a dynamic between two partially contradictory modes. First, *Dracula* tourists are driven by a desire to make a concrete comparison between the landscape they are visiting and their mental image. On the other hand, this rational approach to trace reality is contrasted with a more intuitive, emotional desire for a temporary symbiosis of both worlds. (2011: 231)

Similar to the research outcomes of Brooker, fans differentiate between fact and fiction, yet are driven to somehow shore up the two in real time. Reijnders notes this contradiction:

> Dracula tourists use rational terms to describe their desire to make concrete comparisons between imagination and reality, they are also driven by an emotional longing for those two worlds to converge. What these two modes have in common is their distinctly physical foundation: they are both based on a sensory experience of the local environment. (2011: 233)

Though they intellectually know that events in Bram Stoker's masterpiece are imaginary, there is a longing to find a higher, deeper connection beyond the written word on the page. Brooker argues that there is a yearning to connect not with the actor or even the communities found on social networking platforms, chat rooms, fan forums, and even real-time visits to spaces, but with the text itself in a transcendent, more profound fashion. His respondents repeatedly described their experiences of actually going to spaces where favorite shows and movies were shot as fantastical, 'If a movie is like a dream, then standing in an actual location is like stepping into the dream ... the feeling of connection is not with other fans, but with the fiction' (Brooker, 2005: 25). It is with the characters that inhabit these invented worlds that the fan related to, as the pilgrim was not bonding with other travelers, but was trying to deepen their connection with the mediated figure – 'with Luke Skywalker ... Mulder and Scully ... [fictional protagonist of the Star Wars movie series and leading characters of the X-Files TV show]' (Brooker, 1999: 160). This theory can be carried over to any mythologized figure, whether once living (Ian Curtis, Marc Bolan) or only ever fully realized through a camera lens or an author's pen.

ZOMBIES R US

In 2013, Nicolas Barber wrote, 'It's now more than a decade since zombies began their relentless shuffle into the mainstream of popular culture'. He identified the start of the horror creatures' newly invigorated emergence into media as Danny Boyle's terrifying post-apocalyptic film 28 Days Later. He argues that this new popularity for the matinee fear favorite 'can't be a coincidence ... [as] ... zombies are in vogue during a period when banks are failing, when climate change is playing havoc with weather patterns, and when both terrorist bombers and global corporations seem to be beyond the reach of any country's jurisdiction' (ibid.).

However, I would also suggest that the longevity of this flesh-eating monster trend also rides on how western society has become zombified itself, often lacking the time and head room to process the tsunami of information that is constantly bombarding us via e-mails, cell phones, and virtual lives. Barber contends that the appeal of zombies offers us a source of escapism from our often overwhelming problems of the modern world, many of which are out of our control. He quotes writer Max Brooks, author of *World War Z* (which would later go on to be a cinematic Brad Pitt zombie vehicle), explaining the continued investment by fans with the flesh-eating ghouls, 'zombie stories give people the opportunity to witness the end of the world they've been secretly wondering about while, at the same time, allowing themselves to sleep at night because the catalyst of that end is fictional' (ibid.). Barber believes, however, that the real reason we flock to the fiends is because they are possibly a view of our worst possible selves, as 'they're frightening because of how dismal it would be to become one yourself' (ibid.).

I would argue, however, that the fascination with the zombie is twofold. Objectively, we have been often forced to become zombies ourselves, doggedly following along to the newest trend as set by #Twitter, trying to not drown in a world of instant accessibility and data overload. It is becoming harder and further obscured to differentiate between important and non-consequential, as tabloid, celebrity-driven news battles more detrimental humanitarian issues for space and the attention of punters. At the time of this writing, Zayn Malik, leaving his reality television formed band, One Direction, is sparring off for top billing on newspapers and websites alike with the tragedy of a suicidal co-pilot Andreas Lubitz, who killed himself and all 150 people on board the Germanwings Flight 9525 he was flying. This lack of clarity between fame-inflated sensationalism and true, horrifying tragedy is even further intensified as '1D' fans take to Instagram and Twitter to display their self-harming photos, in a bid to outdo each other at their grief for the singer's departure. Are we zombies? I would say yes, as it is the easiest way to survive the current climate. Zombies are inherently devoid by definition of planning, thinking, rationalizing – all traits which are held high as unique to humanity. Yet these very same characteristics are being sucked continuously away from us in the current climate. In order to keep up and fit in, the path of least resistance appears to be the simplest, to just be swept along with the pack (aka any scene from choose-your-favorite-zombie movie), in the herds of the seemingly brainless moving en masse. While this may sound far-fetched and perhaps a bit harsh as a critique of modernity, it does succinctly describe the social economy where the fate of a celebrity sparks more interest than a true impending crisis.

The zombie parallel may be just an illustration of our desire, per Brooks, to escape from such monumental possible doom; yet the denial of our tentative circumstances leads us back to feasting not on brains but on fiction, instead of confronting pertinent crisis.

This leads to perhaps the other reason for the continued obsession with the flesh-gorging ghouls. A global event – like a zombie apocalypse – would enable us to re-set everything. Ok, I know it sounds mad, but hear me out. Imagine not having to worry about money, status, materiality in any form as we now experience it. To live just to survive sounds somehow refreshing. With all of the pressure to consume, purchase, display, with worth being based almost solely on material prosperity, a little thinning of the proverbial herd and getting back to basics somehow sounds really appealing.

Enter the ever-growing popularity of AMC's television series, *The Walking Dead*.

Writer Robert Kirkham and artist Tony Moore premiered the ongoing black-and-white graphic novel series in 2003. Since then, there have been more than 22 volumes of the comic following the lives of protagonist Rick Grimes, his family, and a group of survivors during a zombie apocalypse. In 2009, television network AMC bought the rights to produce a television show based on the books. The first episode premiered on October 31, 2010, to high ratings. It has since been renewed for six seasons, with the finale of the fifth season premiering in March 2015. Producer David Alpert already has plans for many more episodes of the show, stating,

> I happen to love working from source material, specifically because we have a pretty good idea of what season 10 is gonna be. We know where season 11 and 12 [would go] … we have benchmarks and milestones for those seasons if we're lucky enough to get there. (Tabrys, 2014)

The Walking Dead hails from what is being called the second 'golden age' of television. Formerly, TV was the red-headed step child to the more glamorous and high-profile film world, as 'cinema has historically considered itself superior to television, with executives and critics frequently sneering that a movie or documentary has a "made-for-TV" feel' (Lawson, 2013). However, shows like *Mad Men*, *The Wire*, and *The Sopranos* paved the way for richer storytelling to appear on the small screen. As highly acclaimed director Steven Soderbergh recently said, 'In terms of cultural real estate … TV has really taken control of the conversation that used to be the reserve of movies' (ibid.). *The Walking Dead* has been one of the success stories from this apparent boom time, its intricate storylines drawing increasing market shares. The season five finale of the show broke all its previous records, with 15.8 million viewers in the US, 10.4 million falling into the coveted 18–49 age group (Burlingame, 2015). It is the latest on a blockbuster season for the show, which saw it crush most competitors: 'when including sports and specials, all 16 episodes of *The Walking Dead* season five rank in the top 50 telecasts across all of television among adults 18–49 – the first time a series has achieved this in cable history' (ibid.). It is 'the #1 show in all of television among adults 18–49' (ibid.). Based on the high number of viewers, it is not surprising that fans have begun flocking to some of the locations used on the AMC hit.

Numerous companies offer different packages, allowing for a large choice of what season of the show the visitor wants to focus on. There is even a website, The Walking Dead Locations, aimed at helping the individual in the 'Planning [of] TWD pilgrimage to Georgia' (http://walkingdeadlocations. com). At the time of this writing, there were *seven* different *Walking Dead* tour options, ranging in price from $10 to $65 per person. The most expensive of the lot, the 'Big Zombie' tours ($65), are operated by Atlanta Movie Tours, which 'launched in 2012 with a single "*Walking Dead*"-themed tour. The company now hosts two zombie tours and two other film-related tours and recently welcomed guest No. 10,000' (Hunter, 2014). Each of the tours brings visitors to various locations where specific episodes of the show were filmed. Tour after tour encourages fans to reenact the fictional scenes from the show, thus inserting themselves into the story itself: 'Hold an M16 out the same window Merle did, take part in a zombie bash in the exact spot where Daryl and Martinez did, stand on the spot where Merle appeared as a zombie and go where the Governor sadly killed Merle' (ibid.), as you 'Come walk in the footsteps of the stars' (ibid.).

Real and imaginary co-mingle as pilgrims are further invited to enter and experience *The Walking Dead* spaces not as a staged facade but as an actual, useable place, moving the fantastical experienced on the small screen into a viable, tangible location. Various activities where the show's action took place have been set up to realize *The Walking Dead* world for the fans, as they are persuaded to imbibe in 'Sit[ting] and discuss[ing] the fate of mankind at the old Feed Building, test [their] strength at the Zombie Arena, see the Sportsman's Deer Cooler and Oaks Motor Inn [and] explore Woodbury [the fictional town ruled in season 3 by Grime's arch enemy, the Governor]' (Hunter, 2014).

The impact of this influx of folks to some previously unrenowned locations has had a profound affect on the communities. In Georgia, these 'hardcore fans can bring in millions of tourism dollars when they come to get a firsthand look at the places they've seen on the screen' (Bynum, 2015). According to Lee Thomas, the deputy commissioner in charge of the film division of the Georgia Department of Economic Development, such a 'boost in tourism is one of the greatest economic bonuses the state gets from providing scenery and back-drops to projects from *Deliverance* to *The Walking Dead*' (ibid.). Shows that are 'The biggest hits not only attract fans from overseas', Thomas said, but often route them to small-town locales that wouldn't see many tourists otherwise' (ibid.). Such interest can help a town's economy and 'can be something that carries a town for years and years' (ibid.).

One of these locations is the town of Woodbury, where *The Walking Dead* survivors in season 3 seek refuge in the walled-off community. The main street of fictional Woodbury is actually the downtown portion of Senoia, population 3,750. Over the past decades, residents 'had seen its fortunes fade after the local cotton and agricultural industries died off' (Neely, 2013). A constant influx of fans has dropped onto the town since it was featured on the hit show, res-urrecting it from a derelict state and spawning a 'thriving tourism trade ... where officials say the number of storefronts has grown from six to 47 since the zombies arrived' (ibid.). As plans for a boutique hotel get underway, developer Scott Tigchelaar concedes, 'Ten years ago to talk about a four-star hotel in Senoia, people probably would have laughed me out of town' (Neely, 2013), yet now such accommodation is deemed necessary to support the booming visitor economy. There is even a Woodbury Shoppe, hosting all things *The Walking Dead* – from socks to knives, with pieces from the set, such as the prison cells used in seasons 3 and 4, and a motorcycle replica of the Harley preferred by show zombie killer/heartthrob Daryl Dixon.

Other locals are reaping similar benefits from having been featured in the show. Several business owners can attest to the positive financial impacts the show has had on their enterprises. In his feature on the impact of walking dead tourism, Clay Neely interviewed several stakeholders in and around Senoia. He found that many were 'quick to point out the impact the show has for not only ... business, but for the community as well' (Neely, 2013). One proprietor, Josh Nickell, illustrates the cross-sectional affect of such tourism, claiming,

> If you include the direct and indirect revenue from the production, the impact has been huge ... The production's support of the downtown market and improvement in home values (because of the name recognition of the town) has had a dramatic impact on our revenue. These changes have also allowed us to bring on additional employees in order to keep up with the demand of commercial and residential systems. (Ibid.)

These locations offer some of the best examples of the every day being transformed into the sacred, of meaning being created, maintained, and evolved
via those who have already 'symbolically' made the trip to these sites through
the television show. None of the spots, with the exception of the manufactured
Woodbury Store, are of any note or are particularly memorable. This lacking of
any definitive personality provides an ideal backdrop for the cinematic scope of
The Walking Dead, as the viewer often is focused on the drama instead of the
scenery. It is also reasonable to assume that towns like Senoia have experienced
a rebirth as locations for Hollywood shoots, as its versatile frontage allows it to
be the perfect 'every' or 'any' town USA.

This transformation, from destitute to destination, is magnified by the
worth that pilgrims from all over the world place on attending the zombie
tours. In her report on the areas' rejuvenation, Hunter (2014) notes how when
she visited

> two 'Big Zombie' bus tours drew mostly out-of-state visitors with fans from
> Indiana, Illinois, Michigan, Washington and places across the Southeast, plus a
> fan from Brazil on a monthlong American odyssey, [with] many plan[ning] their
> trips especially to see '*The Walking Dead*' locations up close.

Over on Trip Advisor, many of the clientele often mentioned the tour providing another layer to the viewing of the show, the locations themselves only a
conduit for further integration with the original text. One reviewer notes their
activities once returning from the tour as 'Have since watched T*he Walking
Dead* DVD's all over again and seeing all the places we visited makes viewing
the tv series MUCH more enjoyable!' (Trip Advisor, no date a), while a 'Big
Zombie' pilgrim Mary Kolodziej, about to partake in her second zombie tour
of a getaway weekend, notes, 'Everybody's always like, "What if, what if something happens? I don't know what I would do". Well, the show kind of shows
you what people would do … [as] Everybody can relate to somebody on this
show' (Hunter, 2014). This is arguably the reason that people are so drawn
to the spaces of *The Walking Dead* – it allows the visitor to literally 'walk' the
steps of the relatable fictional characters, bringing the imagined universe of
creator Kirkham to life in real time. By sitting on Daryl's motorcycle, cruising
the streets of Woodbury/Senoia and openly debating the best tactics for survival in case of a zombie apocalypse, pilgrims can integrate their favorite show
into a rehearsal of this fantastical possibility. Kolodziej questioning what her
plan would be in case of such an extraordinary event lends credibility to such
an occurrence being in the realm of the hypothetical, illustrating once again the

ever-decreasing divergence between fictional and real. An interactive map, listing specific sites from all five seasons of the show (https://www.google.com/maps/d/viewer?mid=zD38FaCAJQek.k_FDpSYzC2wl), creates the same sort of virtually 'being there' Crowther recalls in her Google-viewed journey of places pertaining to Plath – once again placing the landscape, characters, and events of the invented show on par with actual space and place.

ONCE A SONG OF ICE AND FIRE

Game of Thrones first appeared on US premium cable channel HBO in 2011. The show, based on a series of fantasy novels called *A Song of Ice and Fire* by George R.R. Martin, quickly gained fans and has been renewed for a sixth season as of this writing. The series interweaves several plot lines, which include weather change, exiled royalty, and civil war in the mythical lands of Westeros and Essos. Much of its success has been attributed to the mainstreaming of the fantasy genre over the last decade, with the powerhouse adaptations of books such as *Harry Potter* and *Lord of the Rings* proving the genre is for everyone, not just paste-eating dorks.

While *The Walking Dead* is shot almost exclusively in and around Georgia, *Game of Thrones* is a globetrotter for location and settings for its fictional world. The sites range from the expected – the US – to a range of more exotic destinations: Northern Ireland, Croatia, Iceland, Morocco, Spain, Malta, Scotland. Additionally, 75% of the show has been filmed at Titanic Studios, located in economically depressed Belfast. A map of the world, available at http://winteriscoming.net/features/filming-map, breaks down specific spots by season, allowing pilgrims to make their way to see where a favorite episode took place. Unlike *The Walking Dead*, the map is not incidental, e.g. it is not organized by crucial moments in particular shows in the painstaking detail attributed to the other virtual directory. While such internet sites allow for mock interaction between space and fan, it also lets individuals cobble together their own guide of key areas and places associated with the show. The existence of a site with this much information points to the demand for this data to be available for potential visitors.

Similar to *The Walking Dead*, in its native US, *Game of Thrones* is gaining ratings every week, crushing the goliath of the main three television networks, especially in the coveted 18–49 age group. Crupi (2015) reports this growth, 'HBO's *Game of Thrones* scared up a staggering 6.95 million viewers, breaking the previous record (6.64 million) it set during the April 6 season premiere'.

The devout are a growing contingent, willing and wanting to take their symbolic Sunday-evening pilgrimages at 9 pm to a different, higher level. The changing viewing behaviors have also allowed for shows such as *Game of Thrones* to garner a larger audience than previously hoped for, thanks to the ability fans have to watch on local networks, stream on various media devices, and use DVD copies of the show to stay caught up.

This has created the opportunity to turn the global view and the economic fortunes of one of the locations, Belfast, from its past of political violence to a destination for tourism and entertainment industry alike. As Rolfe (2014) points out,

> For Northern Ireland's tourism industry, [*Game of Thrones*] represents a huge pool of potential visitors. The province hopes to use the show's popularity to increase the number of tourists to over 2 million annually by 2016, from 1.8 million in 2013 – more than the region's population of just 1.8 million.

Various companies have created coach tours to allow visitors to see first-hand the epic scenery used in the show, such as 'the castle of Winterfell, the seaside cliffs of the Iron Isles and the King's Road leading to the north' (Rolfe, 2014). Unlike the sites used in *The Walking Dead*, which are special for their unremarkable, 'every town-ness', the sites utilized in *Game of Thrones* are specific to Belfast, creating a unique selling point for visitors – 'Fans of the HBO fantasy [will] recognize the landscapes here from the fictional land of Westeros' (ibid.) – instead of having each spot explained as to why it merits a second look, such as the various broken-down, derelict homes that are scattered throughout most episodes of *The Walking Dead*.

The normalcy of such pilgrimage is now almost unnoticeable for its commonplaceness, as even Queen Elizabeth recently took a tour of the Belfast studio where the show is created. Fans from far-flung locations are flooding in to experience first-hand the magic of the *Game of Thrones* vistas. The familiarity with the sites from the show, but also the importance of the relationships, 'like old friends', that Brooker found in his research, is apparent in the reactions of the pilgrims to seeing *Game of Thrones* scenery in person for the first time. Associated Press (2014) notes how:

> Cara and Tom Collins from Springdale, Arkansas, were in Ballintoy Harbour recently to see the rocky coastal setting used in the show for the 'Iron Isles', a kingdom of rugged sailors. 'You can just close your eyes and picture everybody there', said Tom.

Tom's assertion that 'everybody' is there points to the intimate bond felt by fans with both the terrain they have only experienced by the symbolic pilgrimage of viewing the television show and how important – dare I say, familial – the feelings toward the fictional characters are. His use of the informal 'everybody' hints at a close tie, not one of the distance one would normally associate between imaginary and concrete entities.

Besides aiding in creating a booming tourism market, *Game of Thrones*'s northern Ireland production digs have greatly helped shift the sluggish local economy. Belfast is still trying to recover from the 2008 crash and the more recent austerity measures. The presence of *Game of Thrones* has greatly helped in adding jobs and income to the area. According to Associated Press (2014),

> At the end of series four, HBO is estimated to have spent about 87.6 million pounds ($149.1 million) in the local economy in making the show. The benefits are likely much higher when including other factors, such as the knock-on benefits from higher employment.

Game of Thrones has helped reinvent Belfast as a new media hub, as more Hollywood companies begin to see the location and facilities as a possible place of business. One studio, Yellow Moon, located in Holywood – a small seaside village just outside of Belfast which is pronounced the same way as the more glamorous Los Angeles location – has seen a dramatic change in opportunities since *Game of Thrones*. The show has allowed the studio to double their workforce and see a huge upsurge in business and visibility in a relatively short window of time: 'Five years ago, 80 percent of Yellow Moon's work was for local broadcasters, and just 20 percent for productions based in the U.K. or further afield. Now, 70 percent of their work is commissioned outside Northern Ireland' (Associated Press, 2014). Managing Director Greg Darby clearly links the show's popularity to the reverse fortune of the studio: '*Game of Thrones* [is] directly or indirectly responsible for 80 percent of the people that we have taken on in the last three years, because if they [*Game of Thrones*] didn't come we wouldn't have the other work' (ibid.).

It isn't just Belfast and its surrounding areas which are getting a boost from *Game of Thrones*. Other economically depressed European locations are getting a bump thanks to the show as well. In Croatia, the city of Dubrovnik is used as the pivotal capital city of King's Landing in the series. The increase of visitors to this location alone is solely 'responsible for around half of the 10% annual growth in tourists the city has seen in recent years' (Karaian, 2015). These numbers are incredibly crucial for the country's financial well-being, as 'tourism accounts for nearly a fifth of Croatia's economy' (ibid.). Over in Spain, *Game of Thrones*'s utilization of two towns, Seville and Osuna, has already had an almost immediate affect on the community. The boom could not come sooner for a town that boasts an unemployment rate of '34.7 per cent, the highest of Spain's 17 autonomous regions' (Chilton, 2014). One recent on-location shoot in the area drew locals and non-natives alike, as 'more than 86,000 people showed up for auditions', all hoping to land one of the 600 spots for extras needed for the shoot (Rolfe, 2014) – though the gig payed only a paltry £40 per day. In just 'two weeks into filming' there has been a noticeable '15% increase' in tourism (ibid.). Like its EU sibling Belfast, even the short-term shoot of *Game of Thrones* can have long-term affects:

> The tourism information centre in the town has extended its hours since filming began last week to deal with the influx and hotels in a town that is home to 18,000 people. Hotels are fully booked until the end of October, when filming ends, and the town hall is considering setting up a museum dedicated to the series. (Chilton, 2014)

None of these statistics are surprising on their own, and it may be hard to connect how such economic influences impact the spiritual side of life. However, each of these financial successes underpins the validity of each space as not just a site to visit but a place impregnated with worth beyond what is apparent to the casual passerby. This aligns with other, more traditional places of both religious pilgrimage such as Bethlehem and more recent, secular trips to spaces such as Graceland. The place becomes sacred because of the behaviors of not just the visitors but the social apparatus which depend on such attention to support and enhance their own lives and livelihoods.

I DO LIKE TO BE BESIDE THE SEASIDE

Since 2004, *Doc Martin* has graced the small screen across the UK. The show is actually a spin-off featuring a character, Dr. Martin Bamford, first introduced in the 2000 British movie *Saving Grace*. This was followed by two made-for-television 'prequels', which set up the Bamford protagonist as 'just one of the lads', as he smoked, drank, and got down with the local tradesmen of Port Isaac, joining in on fishing and crabbing activities. However, this portrayal did not fly with the network that bought the show. They wanted the good doctor to be a big city slicker with a grumpy disposition who has trouble fitting in to the stereotypically simpler, gentler ways of the Cornish style. With this in mind,

Dr. Martin Bamford became Dr. Martin Ellingham, and Port Isaac, the place where he escapes the big city to fill a vacancy in a local practice, transformed (by name only) into Portwenn. Unlike *The Walking Dead* and *Game of Thrones*, *Doc Martin* has only been shown on a regular basis in the UK, though several other countries, including France, Spain, Germany, Austria, Greece, and the Netherlands, have adapted some of the main ideas and characters to create their own versions, utilizing similar settings native to each country as the fictional 'Portwenn'. While the DVDs of the season have been available in both region 1 (US, Canada, Bermuda, Caribbean compatible) and region 2 (Europe, Middle East, and Japan, among others) formats, the show has not been available globally on streaming services in the same way that *The Walking Dead* and *Game of Thrones* have.

Distribution, availability, and international media push make a huge difference in the reach of a show, and thus in the potential group of pilgrims to visit. Though *Doc Martin* has various other series based on it, these do not necessarily tie into the Cornwall location, characters depicted there, and the storylines associated with the British version. Theoretically, each adaptation of the show will have its own individual places and people crucial for driving the plot line. Thus unlike *The Walking Dead* and *Game of Thrones*, there is not one set of locations for focused attention, as individual translations have their own set of fans. Also, the lack of ability for the show to be easily transported literally by streaming devices massively impacts on the portability and opportunities for new fans to find the show and original fans to keep connected to it, as the ease and convenience of watching has been a factor massively impacting the other two focus case studies. This is confirmed by findings from a study on the motivations of visitors to Port Isaac by Graham Busby and Callum Haines in 2013: 'almost all visitors interviewed [during their research surveys] were from the UK (96%) with only 4% from overseas … the findings show Port Isaac is visited by many loyal repeaters (46.7) although still attracting a healthy number of first time visitors (53.3%)'. This illustrates how the lack of outlets to view the show – thus allowing a symbolic pilgrimage to Portwenn – directly impacts the number of tourists coming to the real Port Isaac. Indeed, Busby and Haines found that

> 277 respondents (91.8%) either agreed or strongly agreed that television programmes actively encourage tourism to the localities featured on screen; whilst 91.1% of respondents stated that they were aware of a television or film location. … This finding supports the argument that imagery depicted in television has a significant subliminal influence upon the viewer and evidently influences their behaviour by inducing them to visit featured localities. (Iwashita, 2008)

Arguably, much of the appeal of *Martin* is the 'fictional' setting of Portwenn and the signs and symbols which are embedded within the show to describe the community. Busby and Haines argue that this is crucial not only in the enduring popularity of *Doc Martin* but in the creation of the idealized vision of Cornish life, as 'when a program obtains a primetime viewing time-slot, as *Doc Martin* [did], it acts as a display window for featured localities' (2013: 108).

Figure 2   Port Isaac, Cornwall, England – the setting for *Doc Martin* and the fictional 'Portwenn'. Photo: Jennifer Otter Bickerdike (2015)

Port Isaac, the coastal village called 'Portwenn' in the show, is as pristine and bucolic as any possible imagined seaside location could be. Busby and Haines (2013: 108) note how 'Images induce certain depictions of an area into the prospective visitors mind, consequently providing them with a pre-taste of the destination' (Fakeye & Crompton, 1991). They see (2013: 109) the transcendence between Portwenn and Port Isaac:

> First impressions of a destination are as likely to come from television as real experiences. Many destinations have inherently attractive physical properties including stunning landscapes and idyllic surroundings. Landscapes are often

compressed through media representations for photographic purposes because visitors are fascinated with pictorial beauty, consequently becoming a commodity for tourism consumption. (Crawshaw & Urry, 2000; Tzanelli, 2003)

A community historically based around the fishing and freight industries since its pier was erected during the reign of Henry VIII, the small hamlet of Port Isaac was further built up in the 18th and 19th centuries. Not much has changed since then, as a stroll through the hilly town is like being transported back in time, with the cobbled streets, stone homes, and absence of modern chain stores, mini-mansions, and 24-hour kebab and fried chicken eateries. It is this lack of modernity, the simplicity of the setting, which is played up in *Doc Martin*, as the locals are as boggled by Ellingham's city ways as he is with the small village pace. There is an appeal to this stripped-back way of life which forces the visitor – while watching the show, but even more so when strolling the streets – to question all the pomp and circumstance we value as necessity. This is what that makes *Doc Martin* as a television show work – the contrast between the serene setting and gentle town folk with the gruff, socially awkward doctor.

Figure 3   *Doc Martin* swag, Port Isaac, Cornwall, England. Photo: Jennifer Otter Bickerdike (2015)

Portwenn and its inhabitants are set as the more authentic way of life against Ellingham's stuffy, uptight bravado. This creates an equation between Portwenn and city life – one of inferred 'real' values while the other perhaps is populated with inflated worth and needless materialism. Within this framework, *Doc Martin*, and especially Portwenn, can be very appealing, as a return, if even for the time of the show or the duration of a visit, to this imagined real.

Ironically, Portwenn is a fictional place, yet by using the actual Port Isaac as the location of the show, any differences between the imaged real and the actual are blurred to almost being inconsequential, as 'commonly television engrosses viewers so strongly that most are not concerned with distinguishing between reality and fiction' (Busby & Haines, 2013: 108). This is not a new phenomenon, as many theorists have noted that film locations are often referred to as 'hyper-real' places of simulation, where reality and artificial components are intertwined and visitors often cannot differentiate between actual and imagined.

This becomes very apparent in the Busby and Haines study. Consisting of 302 people over the course of several days in 2011, the researchers found that

> the majority of visitors (80%) did not seek any information prior to their visit and were largely unaware of any travel-related advertising concerning the locality of Port Isaac (91%). This is significant as it raises the issue of what destination images were held. Did *Doc Martin* have an influence? (2013: 112)

Arguably, visitors already felt as if they had been to Port Isaac from 'being' in Portwenn via *Doc Martin*, thus felt little need to further plan ahead for their trip. Not surprisingly, Busby and Haines (ibid.) found the biggest influence over visiting the village '… was television, with a dominant 42.7%, followed by nostalgia (18.9%) …' (ibid), confirming that television programs actively encourage people to visit the featured destinations, just as previous studies acknowledge. This finding also categorically supports Riley's (1994) suggestion that motion pictures do act as pseudo-tourism attractions, while further inferring that the majority of respondents visit Port Isaac with a preexisting sense of meaning and emotional attachment with the location (Heitmann, 2010; Kim, 2011; Urry, 1990).

The Port Isaac study, like the evidence gathered by examining *The Walking Dead* and *Game of Thrones* tourism, underscores the meaning gathered and nurtured about a place by engaging with a television show or other forms of pop culture fodder. Nostalgia coming in as a second reason for pilgrimage also points to various connotations within the idea – nostalgia for one's own past experiences in Port Isaac, nostalgia for watching the television show at a specific time and/or place, or a combination of these factors, possibly tied in to newer memories cobbled from more recent trips. In this way, the visitor can be nostalgic for a place and time they never visited before – a faux nostalgia that has been created via mediated images and ideas.

This connection was further strengthened by the Busby and Haines statistical findings, showing how impactful media can be for shaping beliefs and values. They reported the

> most significant findings in relation to the aim of this study were firstly that 229 respondents (75.8%) actually associated the case-study location of Port Isaac with a specific image, icon or renowned individual whilst, secondly, these types of reported imagery were largely associated with the physical places depicted within *Doc Martin* (45.4%). This, coupled with the fact that 38 respondents (16.6%) associated Port Isaac with the famous actor Martin Clunes strongly indicates that *Doc Martin* acts as a powerful marketing tool and tourist icon which has been amplified by the involvement of famous actors, thus inducing people to form specific destination images. (Busby et al., 2013; Croy, 2010; Iwashita, 2008)

Importantly, the show not only creates and maintains ideas about the fictional place of Portwenn, then projects them onto the real Port Isaac, it constructs an inauthentic portrait of the folks who live in the real village, as well as the perpetuation of a specific Cornish identity – one laid back, slow-paced, somewhat disconnected from the modern world. This is underscored in *Doc Martin* by not only what is shown – the picturesque landscapes of Cornwall, featuring sweeping oceans, rugged cliffs, and other scenic shots often unabated by the high rises and urban blight that populate many cityscapes – but what it does not show, i.e. the often manic energy, the hustle and bustle of survival in urban life. This paints Port Isaac as an idealized place for pilgrimage, one seeming to offer the chance to recalibrate and prioritize the push and pull of city living while connecting with a simpler, perhaps more wholesome occupant as portrayed by the inhabitants of Portwenn.

However, there seems to be a conflict between this imagined Portwenn and the real Port Isaac in more than name alone. Similarly to sites used in *The Walking Dead* and *Game of Thrones*, the show has created another marketing lever and additional awareness for devout fans, creating an opportunity for the historically deprived county to further drive tourism. Various locations from the show are advertised across the web as key spots to see if one is truly a dedicated *Doc Martin* viewer. The Visit Cornwall website encourages people to 'get your photo taken outside the TV series home of *Doc Martin*, a short way up Roscarrock Hill on the left'

(VisitCornwall.com, no date). The house referred to is the fictional location of Doc Martin's abode; in actuality, it is Fern Cottage, a '2 bedroom self catering holiday cottage' (Doc Martin House, no date) which uses its cache as the 'surgery' from the show as an unique selling point. Fern Cottage clearly relies on the perceived differentiation between the 'old fashioned' values of Cornwall, as captured by *Doc Martin*, and the pressure of city living, as Fern Cottage offers a 'certain way to escape the pressures of modern life in an idyllic location' (ibid.). The rental allows the visitor to literally immerse themselves in the fictional world of the television show, as they stay in the same home featured in the imagined universe of Portwenn. Other spaces, like the village's Bay Hotel, also make use of the visibility created by the television series, boasting at the top of their website, 'The Bay Hotel can be seen as Wenn House in the popular TV series *Doc Martin* set in the fictional village of Portwenn and filmed in and around Port Isaac in Cornwall' (Bay Hotel, no date). These descriptions aide in perpetuating the myth of carefree Cornish living, blissfully ignoring recent statistics which found that 'Cornwall is the UK's poorest region – and is now less wealthy than Poland, Lithuania and Hungary' (DavidCDM, 2014). The county also ranks 'equally with the Welsh valleys as the poorest part of the UK, and is in the top ten most deprived areas in western Europe' (ibid.). This financial predicament makes it even more crucial that the fantasy of Cornish living be upheld against the staggering reality of daily struggle, as visitors brought to the area by secular pilgrimage become an ever more important income stream. This intertwined nature between the imagined idyllic and the pressing monetary reality is further emphasized by the various tours on offer to places associated with *Doc Martin*. For example, the 'Port Isaac & Portwenn Walk & Talk Guided Tours' 'take you around the hidden paths of the village of Port Isaac (Portwenn) taking in *Doc Martin* locations, historical buildings, fishing, past and present' (Port Isaac & Portwenn: Walk & Talk Guided Tours, no date). The lack of any meaningful definition between the actual village (Port Isaac) and the made-up town (Portwenn) points to how critical maintaining the aura of escapism (as offered symbolically through the television when viewers tune in to *Doc Martin*) is to perpetuating traffic. Even the guide, John Brown – native of Port Isaac for 'half a century' (ibid.) – personifies the conflict between idealized Cornish tradition and harsh economic realities. The site depicts Brown as a proper seaside stereotype, noting how he and his family have 'been fishing here [Port Isaac] for as long as reliable records' and that 'John is one of two brothers still fishing along with their sons' (ibid.). This positions him as an insider and strengthens the value of his involvement in 'filming on *Doc Martin*, *Saving Grace* and *Poldark*' (ibid.). His various jobs, however, point to the need for additional income created by media pilgrimage and the plight of indigenous folk in the present economy.

Using Trip Advisor as a further barometer to visitor experience, it becomes clear that there is a rupture between the imagined Portwenn *Doc Martin* and the realities of Port Isaac. While the locals have come to rely on the coverage to generate interest, the facade of perpetuating a fake town within a real community is beginning to show cracks. Many reviewers on the site expressed a deep love for the show, their fandom being the driving factor for the visit, reflecting the findings of Busby and Haines. One writer titled his entry 'Following Doc Martin', underscoring the religious connotations of the visit, as he literally retraces the places seen on the show. Another reviewer exemplified the obscuring between the two villages, proclaiming, '"Port Wen" [sic] is Port Isaac', before describing the day out using the fictional characters and sites instead of the real names and locations:

> We had so much fun, visiting Doc Martins house, the quayside, and wandering around the village. Don't forget that this is a real fishing village, and is a great place to pick up fresh fish for dinner, or to eat it in a restaurant this little village [sic]. Do go up the far hill past Doc Martins house/surgery, and look at the views. (Trip Advisor, no date b)

By referring to the traditional means of employment – fishing – within the context of the imagined show, this reviewer firmly buttresses the fantastical Cornish portrayal as viewed through *Doc Martin*. They sound almost surprised when they find that Port Isaac is 'a real fishing village', as it is depicted on the show. This further entangles the fictional Portwenn with the daily grind of Port Isaac.

Yet many pilgrims wanting to get closer to their own *Doc Martin* mecca were severely disappointed upon arrival, as they looked for the friendly natives of Portwenn in the very real Port Isaac. One Trip Advisor review reported – under the banner title 'Doc Martin has left the village!' – of a less-than-ideal experience. She proclaims, 'The locals are not enamored [sic] of the Doc Martin hype! There was one cafe that sold Doc Martin souvenirs (poor quality & tacky) and the rest of the village don't want to know! A couple of business operaters [sic] were quite rude when we asked about the tv series' (Trip Advisor, no date b). Another Trip Advisor reviewer echoes this feeling of disenchantment between locals and the very tourism trade their community depends upon, noting, 'It would seem that this fame is the bane of the life of the good people of the village as many places were "out of bounds"' (Trip Advisor, no date b). A different entry bemoans a recent visit to Port Isaac, 'NOT MUCH FOR THE TRUE DOC MARTEN [sic] FANS', reporting that 'The places used in the show are easily spotted, but no merchandise is available. Apparently the cast & crew of this show are very rude to the locals and not too welcome!!!' (ibid.).

A recent visit to Port Isaac on a windy, blustering spring day revealed filming taking place throughout the village. Fans, mostly in the over-40 demographic, scurried around, attempting to capture their own picture of one of the actors. As my husband and I sat having lunch, we overheard several groups of pilgrims comparing notes as to who they had seen that day and where. Multitudes trekked up the steep hill at one end of town to have their picture taken outside the private residence that is the frontage for Doc Martin's home in the show. And unlike the Trip Advisor reviewer, I found there to be plenty of Doc Martin flare, from biscuits to badges, stickers to aprons. Maybe the good proprietors of Port Isaac have become more savvy to the full potential of the souvenir market as the show has been renewed year on year.

It is easy to imagine the resentment of Port Isaacians to the invading *Doc Martin* fans. Many a day tripper surely makes more than the average Cornish workers' yearly wage of just £14,300 – almost ten thousand pounds below the national median of £23,300, and almost SIXTY THOUSAND less than the standard inner London salaries of upwards of £71,000 (DaveCDM, 2014). Though they desperately are in need of the influx of cash into the village, locals who may not be directly profiting from the uptick in interest may be left feeling as part of an equation of the haves – the *Doc Martin* pilgrim who can afford such holidays – and the have-nots – the working-class people of the all-too-real Port Isaac.

The common threads between all three destinations is the initial creation of fantastical realities by the television medium, then the attempt by the pilgrim to 'visit' the fictionalized environment in real time – an act of the impossible. Arguably, it is only through the 'symbolic' pilgrimage via the broadcasted show that provides the 'most authentic' version of each of the series, as it is the only place that such a universe truly exists. Any attempt by the tourist to 'step into' the created world of a favorite source material is in vain, as those places, people, and adventures only occur within the perimeters of the small screen. *The Walking Dead*, with its ordinary backgrounds used for an extraordinary story, and *Game of Thrones*'s utilization of breathtaking real place in a pretend universe rely on both the average and the sublime, respectfully, to frame their narratives and move the viewer along on what is obviously a fabricated trip. There is very little likelihood that 'real' zombies will be encountered on a *Walking Dead* tour, or a run-in will occur on site with any of the mythical figures which crowd *Game of Thrones*. This gives even the most 'accurate' pilgrimages to the spaces associated with the two shows an understood nod to participatory imagination, to entering a world which resembles ours but choosing to experience it through the lens of the made-up as assembled by the symbolic.

Doc Martin pilgrims are looking for the same sort of immersion when visiting Port Isaac. Portwenn is just as fabricated as any of the locations showcased in *The Walking Dead* or *Game of Thrones*; however, by so frequently intertwining the two, the very real and historical Port Isaac, with the invented town of Portwenn, they become almost interchangeable and equally 'real' to the visitor. Fans expect to see and interact with the characters from the show, the 'actual' versions of the folks portrayed on the series. Unlike the other two case studies, a visit to Port Isaac is a mash-up and mingling of real and imagined, as costumed *Doc Martin* extras mix with local bar maids, fans, and roving fishermen. The *Doc Martin* swag present in a majority of the shops, the genuine quaintness of Port Isaac, and the unique look and feel of Cornwall from any other place add to the real Port Isaac as Portwenn becomes as seemingly fictional and surely as in flux as any of the sets from *The Walking Dead* or *Game of Thrones*.

2

MR. MOJO RISIN'

More than 40 years after his reported demise, The Doors lead singer, Jim Morrison, has arguably a wider reach now than ever before. The life, death, and evolving legacy of the icon provide a framework to closely examine the complicated and often conflicting ways that pilgrimage, religion, and commodification simultaneously clash and buttress the other. It also shows the spiritual value found by many at his grave, as fans search for meaning and authenticity at a destination that arguably has become a tourist attraction of the most macabre variety. Lastly, the rituals – both sacred and capitalistic – revolving around Morrison create a lens for examining similar behavior in other such sites, namely places tied to the Manchester music scene of the 1970s–1990s and the Marc Bolan Rock Shrine.

Questions still remain and conspiracy theories persist about how and if Morrison actually died. No autopsy was ever performed. Only long-time paramour Pamela Courson and friend Alain Ronay viewed the body before it was sealed in a coffin and buried in Pere Lachaise. The ceremony was quick, with only a handful of people in attendance. According to scholar Peter Jan Margry,

> Five days after Morrison's death on 3 July 1971, despite his global fame as a star he was buried almost anonymously. The grave was nothing more than a nondescript rectangle of sand bound by stone curbs, to which a nameplate was affixed. (2007: 142)

Morrison did not have a proper gravestone until almost ten years after his death. This may be a contributing factor to all of the graffiti on neighboring graves leading to Morrison, as fans tried to create a trail to mark the singer's burial plot for other pilgrims. As Margry notes, 'The social annexation of the space was visible from a considerable distance from the grave and physically marked primarily by the large number of graffiti and inscriptions in and on the trees, graves and mortuary chapels' (ibid.).

Those six missing days – between the last time Morrison was seen alive in public on July 2, 1971, and the shocking announcement in Los Angeles of his passing away on July 8, 1971 – have greatly aided in perpetuating the myth and mystery around not only the person Morrison was in life but the branded commodity he has become through death. Rumors still circulate that he actually died of a heroin overdose at the nearby Rock N Roll Circus nightclub, or that the entire death was staged – that maybe Morrison is still walking among the living. Regardless of the actuality – which will probably never be known, unless the grave at Pere Lachaise is exhumed – all of these stories create a heightened sense of importance of the cemetery site, as a space of not only mourning but of celebration. Both options – of Morrison outwitting the paparazzi to assume a 'normal' life after orchestrating his death; and of the singer being part of the notorious '27 Club', a group that includes Janis Joplin and Jimi Hendrix, both of whom passed away less than a year before Morrison – bolster his larger-than-life, saint-like simulacra. By visiting Pere Lachaise, the fan can convene with these ideas, engaging not only with any actual traits pertaining to Morrison while he was alive but perhaps, more importantly, with beliefs and significance that have been projected onto the singer post-mortem. As Robert W. Kray (2014: 67) writes of the Delta, 'both otherness and authenticity are manifested in a remem-brance and subsequent promotion and performance of a romanticized location and way of life'. This is a repeated motif in other places of sonic pilgrimage, as fans try to recapture an imagined past which may have never truly existed.

Morrison is said to have visited Pere Lachaise shortly before his death and told Courson that it was here he wanted to be buried, 'among the tombs of writers like La Fontaine, Moliere, Proust, and Wilde' (Fitzgerald, 1999). Since Morrison's arrival, the cemetery has been consistently voted one of the top ten spots for tourists to hit when in Paris (Traub, no date). However, it did not take long for 'the French authorities ... to regret their decision [of allowing Morrison to be buried at Pere Lachaise] ... as thousands of fans flocked to visit Morrison's grave – leaving behind empty bottles of Jack Daniels, half-smoked joints, and graffiti' (Fitzgerald, 1999). Margry observes how 'it is the most visited site in the cemetery. The fact that visitor numbers continue to rise in itself points to the peculiar significance of Morrison's grave. It has a meaning that became much broader' (2007: 142). Though hundreds of thousands – possibly a million or more – have been to see the final resting place of the rock legend since his internment, the meaning of who and what Morrison was has been virtually erased.

I first-hand saw this growing and shifting meaning of Morrison within the broader cultural spectrum. On a recent trip to the cemetery on a Wednesday in autumn, more than 75 people stood around the singer's final destination. No one seemed to be paying respects in the way that would be expected at a cemetery – quiet contemplation, leaving trinkets, even playing music or singing songs written by the front man. Instead, guests to the graveyard had maps of Paris's famous city of the dead and were checking off what other occupants of Pere Lachaise were notable 'must sees'. I even overheard several people asking in a variety of languages, 'Who was Jim Morrison?', trying to cobble his place in the wider pantheon of history ('Was he a chef? A comedian?'). There may be more footfall of people coming to see the singer's final resting place – but what exactly are they paying tribute to?

Margry identifies two different kinds of visitors to the Morrison grave: a majority of the people fall into those wanting to lay eyes on what has become 'a major tourist attraction of Paris' (2007: 145). The others are the hardcore Morrison devout who have created a 'cult around the grave of Morrison as an idol and role model' (ibid.). Margry argues that this 'is connected to a broad repertoire of religious rituals and experiences. It is mainly the inner circle of fans that participate in the performance of these practices and rituals' (ibid.) at the site. However, cemetery officials felt that 'everyone should be able to visit the grave' and that the Morrison cult not only were responsible for 'the desecration of the cemetery … [they] kept other people and tourists at a distance' (ibid.). This clash resulted in authorities erecting a metal barrier, barring visitors from physically touching the grave.

MANCHESTER, SO MUCH TO ANSWER FOR: A VERY BRIEF OVERVIEW AND KEY CHARACTERS

> I do not see this as the story of a pop group. I see this as the story of a city, that once upon a time was shiny and bold and revolutionary, and then suddenly, 30-odd years later, is shiny and revolutionary all over again. And at the heart of this transformation are a bunch of groups, one group in particular. – Tony Wilson, *Joy Division* (2007)

Manchester has become mecca for a specific moment in music, a time – not dissimilar to when Morrison was on the scene – when music seemed as if it could change the world. Indeed, the myths and mythology around Manchester – the bands and music culture for approximately a 20-year period, roughly 1978–1998 – did dramatically impact the identity of the north as well as the worldview of the fifth largest city in England. A handful of bands – Joy Division, The Smiths, The Stone Roses, Oasis – and places associated with them – The Factory and the Haçienda – have come to represent the values of not just a moment in music but the possibility of art and the historically disenfranchised to direct the pop media. All four of these bands share not only a heritage of being from the north – the city which forever has lived in the long shadow of capital London – but of conquering the charts and shaping culture for decades seemingly against all odds.

Morrison has become a figure which represents a moment in history, of the late 1960s and early 1970s – experimentation in music, of sexual liberty, and pushing the boundaries of social and expected norms. Like those who seek solace and understanding of the 1960s' optimism at Morrison's grave, pilgrims to spaces and places associated with the halcyon days of 1980s' 'Madchester' and 1990s' 'Cool Britannia', as the press tagged the two epochs, search for what influenced and inspired the bands that they love. Perhaps there is the hope of convening some of the essence to the fans' modern lives as they literally retrace the steps of their idols. Lee Roberts (2014) refers to this phenomenon as 'contagious magic … the properties or qualities associated with the person that in some shape or form are seen to "rub off" on an object or place and to bring about its transformation or symbolic (and by extension economic) revivification'. It is such magic that many of the beliefs and the business of Manchester are based upon.

An easy starting point to this modern pilgrimage industry is the forming of Factory Records, which placed Manchester as a player for the first time on the international music scene. In 1978, local Granada television presenter and quasi-celebrity Tony Wilson began a partnership with friend Alan Erasmus. They decided to start first a nightclub, then a record label, named after Andy Warhol's creative bohemian enclave – Factory – in New York. At the time, most of the players in the UK music business were located exclusively in London, making it a bold statement to entertain success in the northern city. The label's first signing was Joy Division, a post-punk foursome from in and around Manchester. The band and the label's first LP, *Unknown Pleasures*, was released in 1979 and sold out all 10,000 of its original pressings. Amidst the emerging success, tragedy struck in May of 1980 when lead singer Ian Curtis committed suicide at his home in nearby Macclesfield. This pivotal moment is reenacted in 2002's movie about Factory Records, *24 Hour Party People*, when Wilson – played by Steve Coogan – looks straight into the camera and proclaims Curtis as a 'prophet of urban decay … the musical equivalent of Che Guevara' (*24 Hour Party People*, 2002). Curtis's band mates picked up the pieces left from his death and went on to form New Order. While on an early tour of the US, New Order was blown away by the dance music scene at clubs such as New York's Danceteria and Paradise Garage. Using their new inspirations, Factory

Records, New Order, and Wilson built the Haçienda, a nightclub named after a slogan of the radical group Situationist International. Through the Haçienda, the Factory folk attempted to create a vibe similar to those they experienced on the East Coast, but tweak it to reflect Manchester. The venue went on to be ground zero for the 'Madchester' scene, the birth of rave and house music in the UK. Many documentaries and movies have been made about this northern soundscape, including *24 Hour Party People* (2002), *Control* (2007), *Shadowplayers: The Rise and Fall of Factory Records* (2006), and *Joy Division* (2007). Each of these films aides in continuing the legends around the time period, the importance of the key players, and the influence of the artists' impact, arguably reenvisioning all of the notable names as revolutionaries who genuinely shifted not only the fate of Manchester in the 1970s from – as Tony Wilson (*Joy Division*, 2007) described – a 'really grimy and dirty, a dirty old town' to '[being] shiny and revolutionary all over again'.

While Factory was experiencing its own growing pains, The Smiths were starting their short but legendary journey as the original heart on sleeve, shoe-gazer band. Combining the jangly guitar of Johnny Marr with the tongue-in-cheek, personal lyrics of lead singer Morrissey, the band recorded four albums and created a new sound and aesthetic in the five years (1982–1987) they were together. Hailed post-break-up as being 'one of the UK's most successful, significant acts' (Blistein, 2014) and celebrated as having the 'greatest album of all time' by *NME* in 2013 (with *The Queen Is Dead*), the group's impact has lasted decades longer than they existed as a foursome.

Just two years after The Smiths' break-up, The Stone Roses released their self-titled debut album. The record went on to garner top ten singles with songs such as 'Fool's Gold' and win numerous *NME* readers' polls in 1989, with accolades including Best New Band, Single of the Year (for 'Fool's Gold'), and Band of the Year. The group went on to headline Spike Island on May 27, 1990, playing to a crowd of over 27,000. The show has become so infamous in music circles that its importance 'stretches so far beyond the gig itself and music' (Noel Gallagher, *Live Forever: The Rise and Fall of Brit Pop*, 2003). Spike Island has become memorialized as the uniting concert for a cultural moment, garnering comparisons to capturing the nation's mood in a similar means to Woodstock for the generation before. However, commercial success was short-lived, as a second album, the daftly named *Second Coming*, released in December 1994, failed to have the success of the first record. Band infighting, personal issues, and an aborted tour eventually took the toll on the group, which officially broke up in 1996 (yet as of this writing were back together). The band influenced many young musicians, including Noel Gallagher, who went on to form Oasis with his younger brother Liam. Oasis became one of the best-selling bands of the 1990s, leading a new, British-centric music movement called 'Cool Britannia' by the press. After many disputes between the brothers, Oasis broke up permanently in 2009.

These bands all share the characteristics of having rabid fan bases which continue to grow and thrive decades beyond their inception and demise. Often the spaces and places associated with the group while they were active are the only physical contact with the artists available to a secular traveler. A visit to Manchester, therefore, transforms for a fan from a fun day out to be 'perceived as a responsibility, an obligation, a mission and a pilgrimage rather than a mere opportunity to gaze at cultural otherness' (Fry, 2014: 75). Indeed, instead of feeling such 'otherness', participants on tours often feel a sense of connectivity, with the text of the songs and their writers (as noted by Brooker in Chapter 1) as well as with others who have made the trek before them. In this manner, 'fans undergo a transformative process in which, through an increase in cultural and social capital … fans … become … temporarily of the host culture' (ibid.) – even if this 'host culture' only currently exists in the reimagined stories from the past.

DOUBLE-DECKER BUS

It is now commonplace for 'tourism and cultural agencies in some English provincial cities … [to promote] their popular music "heritage" … through the packaging of trails, sites, "iconic" venues and festivals' (Long, 2014). Now various tours offer to escort the pilgrim to the key spots where former incidents of greatness took place in and around Manchester. The most prolific company, Manchester Music Tours, is run by Craig Gill, drummer from Madchester luminaries Inspiral Carpets (the band in which Noel Gallagher himself worked briefly as a roadie before finding fame in Oasis). On offer are several different walks, each focused on a specific iconic band – Joy Division, The Smiths, The Stone Roses, Oasis – with a fifth, the 'Manchester Music Walk', providing an overarching whistle stop of locations pertinent to key moments in Manchester music history.

Manchester Music Tours originated from Gill's own experiences interacting with visitors to the northern stronghold who were specifically looking for key locations they had only read about or seen pictures of. He remembers being asked repeatedly,

> Is the Haçienda still there? How do you get to the Salford Lads Club? So I handed people little badly drawn maps and told them which buses to get on. I had visions of these Japanese tourists with their big cameras getting lost around Salford and Hulme. (Roue, 2015)

Gill's insider knowledge of and passion for the Manchester music scene turned into the business, which has 'welcome[ed] visitors from all over the world and double[ed] ... turnover to £30,000 in the last 12 months' (ibid.). His pedigree as not only a member of the Madchester scene but a native Mancunian provides perceived added value to many fans, as 'the possibility of hearing, seeing, or interacting with something genuine [locals] ... provides one opportunity for a unique and meaningful encounter ... meaningful experiences also manifest through "authentic" interactions with the space, people and music' (Fry, 2014: 75).

Roberts, who took Gill's tour, recalls how the specific tales shared by the drummer highlight and buttress the legends of the city's soundscape:

> Rather than offering a straightforward historical chronology of the post-punk scene in Manchester, the narrative largely comprised a number of clearly well-rehearsed anecdotes and stories. Many of these were the guide's own memories of attending gigs, clubs and performances in Manchester ... The interweaving of the guide's peripatetic narrative style with the locations and routes that meandered their way through sites of post-punk musical memory had the effect of mythologizing the music city. (2014: 22)

It is imperative that anecdotes shared during the tour dovetail with the pilgrims' understood value of the place and spaces visited – indeed, ideally the experience should deepen the meaning and beliefs inferred from the tour. Kirshenblatt-Gimblett (1995) notes the importance of this as 'they [visits to such perceived sacred spaces] transport tourists from a now that signifies hereness to a then that signifies thereness. The attribution of pastness creates distance than can be traveled'. Gill would endanger not only his fledgling business by revealing any new 'thereness' that deviated from the well-loved (and well-known) narratives but also threaten to unravel the now accepted history of the city.

Gill has also co-written a book with Phil Gatenby, *Manchester Musical History Tour* (2011), chronicling the different routes for sale by his company in a text form. Gatenby is responsible for putting together one of the first comprehensive guides to locations pertinent to The Smiths. In 2002's *Morrissey's Manchester: The Essential Smiths Tour*, Gatenby painstakingly details each and every site in and around Manchester associated with the band. He lists tiny minutiae, with directions on how to create one's own pilgrimage to these crucial scenes of Smiths' history. Literally bus routes, steps needed to take, and coordinates are included along with a map – making this DIY pilgrimage a personal journey, assisted by Gatenby's knowledge of the area. His 'essential' stops are comprehensive, with thorough directions for accessing specific places, even entreating the fan to visit sites which are no longer there – such as the Haçienda, which has been flattened and rebuilt into luxury apartments, any semblance of the original remaining in name alone (and a small piece of the club's dance floor on display in the building's foyer).

Figure 4   What is left of the Haçienda nightclub is in name alone – luxury apartments where the infamous club used to stand in Manchester, England. Photo: Jennifer Otter Bickerdike (2008)

Figure 5   One relic from the original Haçienda nightclub – a small piece of the dance floor now displayed in the foyer of the apartment building of the same name. Photo: Jennifer Otter Bickerdike (2008)

This allows the visitor to engage once again with nostalgia for a moment only described but not often actually experienced by the individual. Thus the feelings of longing for a past which appear – via the books and the tours, whether self-guided or purchased through Gill – are underscored. As the reader follows Gatenby's map, they stand here in front of a chain outlet of Subway sandwich shop, which was once an indie record store employing Johnny Marr, there a club the band played at once stood, now home to a burgeoning estate agent. Roberts argues, 'Performativity in the context of the heritage trail denotes a more active and participatory mode of urban cultural and spatial practice: memory-work in which the tourist re-creates, re-treads, re-inscribes and re-inhabits spaces of popular music memory' (2014: 23).

   The seeming possibilities on offer from the space and time described on these tours – a moment where art and culture were booming and indie communities were thriving – are a bold contrast to the capitalistic, large conglomeration landscape which meets the pilgrims' eye today – thus once again enforcing the equation of the past as something to be valued and cherished, much like an exotic insect caught in amber.

CAPITALIZING ON CREATIVITY

It is not new for a city to utilize its musical heritage as a driver for tourism, playing on the fan communities' increased worth placed on specific icons. For decades, Liverpool has used what Roberts calls the 'pull factor' (2014: 23) of hometown heroes the Beatles as an important source of revenue for the city.

Figure 6   'The Beatles Story' in Liverpool, England. Photo: Jennifer Otter Bickerdike (2011)

The UK as a whole is now attempting to capitalize on its musical past, as national organizations such as Visit Britain and England Rocks! are including such heritage sites at the heart of marketing initiatives. Roberts notes how such campaigns

> [seek] to capitalize not just on places associated with particular artists, but also places featured in songs ... the campaign [was] ... at its most effective when able to market sites that were marked in some way or had a physical and tangible presence, so as to allow it to function more effectively as a viable visitor attraction. (2014: 18)

Here the direction shifts from attempting to (re)capture a feeling and/or create a moment reflecting the communal shared nostalgia for a specific song, artist, or event to wanting to pin down this ethereal value to a definitive place which can drive commerce. Roberts reports how this marks a change, from the music scenes literally being just a part of a city's narrative to a directly capitalistic value. He notes how

> The focus [of national marketing campaigns] [were] on tangible things that you could pay for or go and see, even if it was a blue plaque on a building, like [with] Jimi Hendrix ... *something tangible that people could go to* [authors italics] ... the growth of tangible music heritage sites that is evident in the United Kingdom is an indicator of the way city and regional authorities have sought to exploit the symbolic capital offered by local popular music geographies. (Roberts, 2014: 19)

However, there is an inherent tension in marketing cultural principal. While it could easily be justified as celebrating and sharing musical heritage, there also is 'understandable desire by city marketing agencies to engage tourism promotion while claiming "hidden gem," "below the radar" status' (Long, 2014: 62). It is hard to share such 'secret' locations and have them remain valued for their inherent obscurity and exclusivity. Long also notes the paradox and challenges of balancing such 'artistic sensibilities and "official" City discourses and the enlisting of musicians and artists as city marketing "ambassadors"' (ibid.), quoting Mallinder's (2011: 82) statement that there are 'inherent problems of institutionalizing popular cultural forms and a resistance of sound to being anchored and contained'.

Music has historically been the enclave for revolt, the haven for the rebel. Such commodification threatens to destroy this space as it has formerly functioned, from one of sanctuary – thus inspiring the secular pilgrimage – to one of mechanized product. This is specifically precarious in scenes such as the ones 'toured' by Manchester Music Tours, as their value depends on ideas of DIY authenticity and cultural change, both of which come under threat as their worth moves from intangibly referential to a 'viable visitor attraction'. In his article on the busking practice at the Cliffs of Moher, Adam Kaul highlights how 'the relationship between cultural values and commercial development is fraught with tension ... [as] ... the simplified public discourse content that what was once a national [public] resource is now a commodified tourist product' (2014: 36). Thus whether it is a national initiative as pushed by bodies such as England Rocks!, Visit Britain, or independently run ventures such as Gill's Manchester Music Tours, the meaning and memory of not just a specific place but an entire cannon of musical importance is shifted to fit the money-making needs instead of a personal set of values and beliefs. In a fan economy where 'ideas of authenticity are rooted not only in notions of the past but also in the present act of participation' (Fry, 2014: 71), any impedance could destroy not only the commerce received from visitors but the very 'genuine' experience which provides much of its understood value to pilgrims, as 'many fans perceive their visit as a homecoming' (74).

STRANGE DAYS

While Pere Lachaise is bang in the middle of one of the most bustling metropolises in the world, the Marc Bolan Rock Shrine is located in the Greater London suburb of Barnes, a leafy, upper-middle-class enclave where a recent, new-build studio apartment went on the market for a cool £1 million. The particular spot is significant, however, as the Shrine is built at the spot where, in 1977, the car in which the singer was a passenger spun out of control, hit a steel-reinforced post before coming to a stop at a sycamore tree on the median. Bolan, lead singer of Tyrannosaurus Rex (T. Rex) and international glam rock pioneer with songs like 'Bang a Gong (Get It On)' and '20th Century Boy', died from head injuries sustained during the tragedy. As soon as the accident was reported, the site became a place of pilgrimage for Bolan fans worldwide. One such visitor was Fee Warner, who began making trips to the site in September of 1977. For over two decades, Warner regularly visited what was then referred to as the 'Bolan Tree' to tidy up any decaying tributes and check on the precarious state of the sycamore, which had been badly damaged in the crash. Though being a focal space of international interest, the 'Bolan Tree' was often in disarray, being described in a 'Glossy Magazine article in 1995 as "More like a shit-hole than a shrine" because of the litter & general air of neglect at the site' (marc-bolan.org, 2015).

The fortunes of the site changed, however, when in 1999 Warner formed T. Rex Action Group – TAG – in reaction to a report that the sycamore tree was in danger of being felled. TAG saved the tree and began its quest to preserve the space, create a permanent shrine to Bolan, and continue to celebrate his musical legacy. Now, more than 15 years since its inception, TAG has managed to keep the site clean, lay steps going up and down from a constructed platform where the tree was located, and even dedicate a bronze bust of Bolan (paid for exclusively by Warner) at the space. The Shrine has become a remembrance site for other members of T. Rex and their luminaries who have passed away, with five other memorial plaques being installed in and around the Shrine. Colorful ribbons, flags, and feathers along with the plaques arguably change a non-descript patch of road into a place with persuasive meaning.

Figure 7   The tree of Marc Bolan's fatal accident, once part of the Marc Bolan Rock Shrine, Barnes, England. Photo: Jennifer Otter Bickerdike (2011)

The success and staying power of TAG and the Shrine as a place of pilgrimage is arguably down to Warner and her dedication of time, money, and enthusiasm for maintaining the space and the legacy of Bolan. Warner calls out a common issue with fan communities, that of big talk with little movement, a situation which has been exacerbated by the ease of 'liking' and sharing information on social media without having to exert any effort or energy. On the marc-bolan.org site, Warner describes the formation of TAG: 'The word "ACTION" was crucial because many people had "talked" of "doing something" for many years, but nothing had actually ever been done!' Though Warner has dedicated many hours,

MARC BOLAN
25th Anniversary
16th September 2002
Sad to see
Them mourning you
When you are here
Within the
Flowers & the Trees
Donated to TAG
by Fee Warner

Figure 8   Bronze bust of Bolan at the Marc Bolan Rock Shrine. Photo: Jennifer Otter Bickerdike (2011)

pounds, and emotional investment to the space and to TAG, she has also smartly made sure that legally the Shrine is the responsibility of the organization, not herself as an individual. On marc-bolan.org, she clearly confronts any criticism which could arise as to one person holding such a great stake in the primary place of remembrance for Bolan, as she publicly posts details about the lease of the property where the Shrine is located:

The accompanying literature gave TAG Full ownership & Responsibility for the 'Bolan Tree' itself. The lease is made out to TAG not to Fee Warner or any individual. This was at the specific wish of Fee Warner and is crucial for the long-term care of Marc Bolan's Rock Shrine. As long as TAG exists, the lease will continue. This allows the site to be cared for over generations. This would not have been the case had the lease been made out to an individual.

While there are numerous other sites dedicated to Bolan on the net, including The Official Marc Bolan Fan Club, Marc Bolan Music, and The TOMB – The Official Marc Bolan Resource Centre, none of them mention TAG, Warner, or the Rock Shrine, making it appear that there may be infighting among this niche community as hinted at on TAG's site. TOMB has a map to what they refer to simply as 'The Tree', tagging the directions themselves as 'Local Map to "Gipsy Lane" the place of the Crash' (tilldawn. net). TOMB is mainly a directory for all things Bolan related, listing cover bands, rare recordings, and pretty much every imaginable possibility connected even slightly to the late singer – except any information on Warner's group and the status of the Shrine itself. TOMB underlines this exclusion in their 'About Us' section, clearly throwing shade on Warner and TAG, as the TOMB site founders rant:

> In the past 7 years we have watched the net become – in some sad instances – a place of rivalry and attempts at 'owning our Dear Marc's Name' that is NOT the case here ... Marc isn't here and he surly [sic] has NOT given us nor anyone the permission [sic] to call their site *OFFICIAL WEBSITES ... We would not be pompus [sic] enough to think that we or *anyone has Marc's Blessing with that said call yourself what you will – hopefully in the same spirit – but above all just keep the sites informative and free of division and attempts at owning something that none of us could nor should try and own the GIFT of Marc's Music. ... Thats all Folks [.]*

Though they claim to not be decisive in their site and fandom, TOMB is obvious in their disdain for Warner's/Marc Bolan Rock Shrine/marc-bolan.org's title of 'TAG Official Marc Bolan and T. Rex Site'. Instead of uniting in adoration for the fallen icon, fans seem to be splintered over who has rights to what memory and commemoration.

In May 2015, the very tree that TAG had been formed to rescue had to be felled. In late 2014, an unknown person ripped out the heart of the tree and poured poison into the hole, killing all of the new sapling sprouts that TAG had been nurturing in an effort to resurrect the sacred sycamore. In April 2015, TAG members arrived at the tree to find saw marks on the trunk, where again someone had tried to unsuccessfully cut down the landmark. When TAG repre-sentatives returned to the tree on May 11, 2015, they found

> fresh saw marks in a different place, but all were low down by the base of the Bolan Tree. The person/persons unknown had taken the saw to the site to cut off and take away all the side shoots of the Bolan Tree. Many of these side shoots had tributes on them and these were also taken. (http://us2.campaign-archive2.com)

The damage was so severe that there was no choice but to cut the tree down for safety reasons. Now a barrel rests over the remains of the Bolan Tree, and fans have already began using this to affix homages. However, the reason-ing behind the purposeful destruction of the tree is unclear and can only be hypothesized that it may have been done by another fan angry at the efforts of TAG and their arguable 'ownership' of the place and Bolan's legacy, or perhaps even a local resident tired of the feathered adorned branches arching over the road.

While some followers use the internet to publicly post their grievances toward each other, TAG uses its site to post an online list of Bolan preservation efforts, including various fundraising, awareness campaigns, and legal pursuits that TAG has had to undertake in order to preserve the Shrine, keep Bolan in the cultural conversation (such as doggedly pursuing the naming and cre-ation of a Marc Bolan rose!), and perhaps, more importantly, continue to have working relationships with nearby neighbors, who understandably could have concerns about possible behaviors at the Shrine. Even the gratuitously mean actions taken against the tree did not draw any online backlash from TAG, which instead just posted the bare facts of the incident leading to the tree coming down. TAG also uses its web presence to remind fans to be considerate and suggest appropriate behavior when visiting the Shrine.

It is easy to envision some of the worries that Barnes locals may have about visitors to the site. Margry notes how Morrison's grave is 'increasingly ... the central physical reference point for fans and devotees from around the world' (2007: 142). He goes on to explain, 'The collision between the Morrison cult and the order of the cemetery is most clearly visible at the material level' (ibid.), in the trinkets, flowers, and other homages that fans leave at the grave. The barrier at the burial spot has been 'an intervention that has inverted the mean-ing and functions around [Morrison's] grave' (141), as 'the physical presence at the grave and the possibility of making full contact made the ritual of touching central' (145) to the pilgrim. The actions and customs have been forced to change because of the security – not because of an organic shift in the meaning of Morrison. The fan experience and their expectation of a visit to the grave are, therefore, greatly altered. One pilgrim interviewed by Margry felt that because of the new configuration at the site,

> she experienced mental and physical exclusion from the person she was coming for. The fencing and the permanent surveillance by policeman and functionaries of the cemetery made it impossible for anyone to touch or stroke the grave and to have the bodily experience of proximity to the grave and physical contact with the sacred place … ma[king] it difficult to experience the right feeling at the grave. (2007: 141)

Such precautionary measures at the grave create a curated version of retrospect and homage, as dictated by the limited access to the actual stone, making the connection and meaning provided by the grave radically transformed. This has perhaps aided in the disintegration of Morrison's meaning for a large contingent of those seeking some of his 'contagious magic' via his final resting place.

While Marc Bolan's remains[1] are not at the Shrine, the proximity to where he spent his last seconds of life provides an equally compelling space for contemplation. Richardson states how crucial it is for individuals to be able to leave items at a grave or a place of special meaning, as 'The leaving of artifacts helps people to establish the location as a place' (2001: 266). Unlike Morrison's highly guarded grave in a public space where fans are prohibited from interacting with the sacred grounds, the Shrine is accessible to anyone willing to make the trek out to Barnes and participate in homage to the rocker. Upon arrival, they are greeted with a tidy yet colorful space. Before being felled, the sycamore tree was always decorated with feather boas, notes, cards, and pictures, all in various stages of decay from the rainy English weather. A notice board allows fans to neatly leave remembrances, many which consist of pictures of the singer, thanks for his contributions and even drawings. One visitor to the Shrine reported that such a variety of tributes

> giv[es] the memorial a deeply personal angle that is often lost in more formal settings. It is quite moving to read the messages and poems left by fans who have travelled from all over the world to visit the shrine. One plaque was left by a visitor from Zimbabwe; another message was left by a fan from Ecuador. (Caroline, no date)

---

[1]   He was cremated; his ashes are now marked by a plaque where they are interred in London's Golders Green Cemetery.

A variety of other affects round out the material offerings at the shrine. A smattering of white swans – a reference to the T. Rex song 'Ride a White Swan' – as well as a myriad of witchy, pagan-flavored bits and pieces mentioned throughout Bolan's work are fastidiously laid out in and around the site. The order of the shrine is a glaring contrast to similar spaces, such as Ian Curtis's grave in Macclesfield.

Figure 9   The grave of Ian Curtis in Macclesfield, England, overflowing with flowers on the anniversary of his death. Photo: Jennifer Otter Bickerdike (2012)

Figure 10   The grave of Ian Curtis, one month after the 30th anniversary of his death.
Photo: Jennifer Otter Bickerdike (2012)

Depending on the month and time of year, Curtis's 'kerb' is overflowing with
bright flowers or resembling a compost pile. Unlike the Barnes location, there
is no regular maintenance and upkeep of the singer's grave, making it appear
visited but uncared for. The Marc Bolan Rock Shrine, on the other hand, most
likely because of its situation in a highfalutin area, is extremely tidy; even older,
fading letters and illustrations are carefully ordered on the board, creating the
overall affect of glittery remembrance instead of haphazard homage.

The English Tourist Board officially recognized the Shrine in 2007, when it was
included in their England Rocks! guide to 'Sites of Rock "N" Roll Importance' – an
honor only bestowed singularly to Jimi Hendrix and Freddy Mercury previously.
Arguably it is the commitment of TAG, Warner, and other Bolan devotees who
have transformed a place of tragedy into a place of celebration.

3
FOR THE LOVE OF BLOOD SUCKERS

> For a moment or two I could see nothing, as the shadow of a cloud obscured St. Mary's Church. Then as the cloud passed I could see the ruins of the Abbey coming into view, and as the edge of a narrow band of light as sharp as a sword-cut moved along, the church and churchyard became gradually visible. It seemed to me as though something dark stood behind the seat where the white figure shone, and bent over it. What it was, whether man or beast, I could not tell. – Bram Stoker, *Dracula* (1897)

Television and film provide the visual landscape for the viewer, drawing them into a different world with a specific, defined set of perceptible cues. There is no mystery as to what is on the screen; even shows like *The Walking Dead*, where the nondescriptness of the scenery is crucial to creating a specific tone for the show, depends on the nonverbal brushstrokes of meanings supplied by the rural backdrop. Music provides the lyrics and often the artist to fill in any additional backstory of a particular song or album, once again providing the consumer with an often prefabricated context. Books, however, depend on the reader using their imagination to become immersed in the story; even the most detailed description in a text is often open to interpretation, creating the opportunity for a special connection between text/character and reader. Squire sums this up, noting how 'literature is a social construct; a vehicle through which both writers and diverse readers negotiate meaning of values for places' (1996: 76). Similar to journeys made to spaces associated with favorite television shows or bands, literary pilgrimage is the proverbial 'next step' in getting closer to a beloved media. Herbert views literary pilgrimage as being 'a merging of the real and the imagined which gives such places a special meaning' (1996: 77). It is a way for the reader to make sense of not only the text but of why and how it has come to have such deep-held meaning in an individual's life.

Stijn Reijnders (2011) examined the motivations of fans to spaces and places related to Bram Stoker's *Dracula*, particularly in Transylvania. Stoker's writing in the classic gothic tale is extremely vivid, painting a scene of exotic depravation: 'a land of howling wolves, vampires, bats and gloomy castles' (2011: 231). Reijnders writes,

> The descriptions of [*Dracula* protagonist Jonathan] Harker's are so thrilling and visual that they acquired a permanent place in the popular imagination, thanks in part to the many re-prints of the novel but also the innumerable screen versions that appeared throughout the twentieth century. (Ibid.)

As the fan visits favorite television show locations, Reijnders found that '*Dracula* tourists are driven by a desire to make a concrete comparison between the landscape they are visiting and their mental image' (ibid.) of the places described in the book. Folks want to see if the scenery they have created in their minds measures up to actual spaces and places. This desire is so strong that fans have warped and created parallels between unrelated actual monuments in the region, located on the west side of Romania. Reijnders notes how 'Stoker's description of Harker's journey is both detailed and geographically well-informed, which made it possible for ... tourists to repeat large parts of the journey step by step. And where Stoker's descriptions provided insufficient detail, the tourists are happy to fill in the gaps themselves' (2011: 232). He specifically sites the transformation of Bran Castle – a building located 'several hundred kilometers' from where Stoker described the location of the vampires lair – into *the* Dracula castle. There was never a castle in the spot that Stoker describes in the book; it was a creation of his imagination. Yet as 'fans were ... eager to at least find a castle' (2011: 231), Bran – by location, looks, and remoteness – *became* Dracula castle. Reijnders points out how easy it was for this leap from real to actual to take place, as 'Bran Castle was in a location that was easy for the tourists to reach, and its restored Gothic style was a good fit with the image tourists had of what Dracula's castle should look like' (ibid.). So keen were pilgrims to find *a* castle that they literally turned an unrelated location into *the* location, transforming the fictional to the real (Bran Castle becoming transposed and morphed onto Dracula castle). While Reijnders admits that 'The fact that this was not the "authentic" location was perhaps a disadvantage' (ibid.), he also shows how the desire to pin the beliefs and value of the *Dracula* story on a concrete location (like Graceland does for the Elvis myth) outweighs the need for the place to be completely credible. The castle's new-found lineage also 'illustrates how the significance of sights is constructed as much by the tourists' (Light, 2007: 754–55) as by what is presented as the actuality. Rojek underscores this, as 'it should not be assumed that either the factual or the fictional have priority in framing the sight. Rather, sight framing involves the interpenetration of factual and fictional elements to support tourists orientations' (1997: 53). The orientation, in the evolution of Bran castle, is the importance and value that pilgrims have placed on there being a 'Dracula's castle', regardless of the very searched-for authenticity. Though the words and text of a book are fixed, the meaning and role that a text can play in establishing self as 'a peoples literary canon is integral to individual and collective identity, and is a source of symbolism, self-determination, and ... pride' (Squire, 1996a: 75). In many studies of literary tourism, such 'realness' of place, space, and objects is highly valued in validating not only the attached attraction but the interest in the site. However, though the words themselves do not change, the 'literary meanings are not fixed. Once texts are created, their meaning are inevitably transformed by readers whose interpretations will be influenced by such varied factors as space, time, age, social class and gender' (Squire, 1996a: 87). The literary pilgrims, however, in the case of *Dracula*, are both sticklers for the details laid out in Stoker's book – as the fictional tale has acted as a detailed map for visitors for decades – but are also willing to allow for a deviation, a flexibility in such truths as written in the book, if it allows for a more immersive, e.g. more fulfilled journey. The fan wants to find intersections in the 'actual' life of everyday Victorians and the fictional world created in the book. Yet they simultaneously want to cobble together any crumbs of seeming likeness between physical places and events with the Dracula story, disregarding the often tenuous at best connections between history and literature. Reijnders points out this contradiction, as Stoker's comprehensive writing presents an outline for the devout, as to the way the different scenes of the book – places, travel, even food – would have appeared in the 19th century. He notes,

> The *Dracula* films and the book are carefully sifted for information: references to existing place names are checked, the travel routes described are traced on the map, and departure and arrival times are compared with official travel times, preferably historical sources from the late 19th century. (2011: 239)

The fact that Bran has come to be 'one of the tourists highlights of the region and, despite the dubious nature of the claim, is widely known as *the* Dracula

Castle' (ibid.) once again proves that the desire to believe is stronger than sensible thinking – yet another parallel between religion and this sort of secular fandom.

Another finding of Reijnders dovetails with the pilgrimages already discussed: how any 'rational approach to trace reality is contrasted with a more intuitive, emotional desire for a temporary symbiosis of both worlds [the lived-in and the one existing within the pages of a book]' (ibid.). Though the visitor knows intellectually that *Dracula* is fictional, there still is the categorical need to know more, to get closer, to enter the text as Brooker argues – even at the cost of the very authenticity which is so deeply craved being lost. It is more important to have a place and be able to literally step into the book's location than it is for the place to have any real connection with the text. The space underscores the visitors' values of the book, as 'the instant when the world of the imagination coincides with – or possibly contrasts with – physical reality. It is this essential to penetrate the world of imagination this media tourist brings along' (Reijnders, 2011: 234).

Figure 11   The ruins of Whitby Abbey, Whitby, England. Photo: Jennifer Otter Bickerdike (2011)

Reijnders's work supports the idea that such travels are very personal and very important on the quest for one's identity. He points out that 'While Stoker used existing surroundings and local history to create his story, the *Dracula* tourist take[s] the story itself as their point of departure, proceeding to search for signs of reality in the story' (2011: 239), hence looking for ways to buttress and substantiate the individual importance placed on the book. This aspect is even more apparent upon visiting the other featured setting of *Dracula*, the North England fishing town of Whitby. Here Stoker set a memorable and crucial scene: on the cliffs overlooking the town, where the ancient ruins of Whitby Abby still stand.

The pilgrim can wander about the graves at the adjacent St. Mary's Church, another location mentioned in Stoker's masterpiece as the place where the vampire hides – after running up the nearby 199 stairs in the form of a dog.

Here the fan may literally walk in and on the steps of the fictional characters – reenacting the story in real time. Similar to pilgrims going to places viewed in their favorite TV show or sung about by a beloved band, the sights and sounds of the

Figure 12   The graveyard next to Whitby Abbey. Photo: Jennifer Otter Bickerdike (2011)

Figure 13   The famous 199 stairs of Whitby, England. Photo: Jennifer Otter Bickerdike (2011)

Dracula landscape, Reijnders argues, have already been experienced via the physical text. He notes,

> for the *Dracula* fans, their visit to Whitby is, in a certain sense, not their first encounter with the town, but rather a renewed encounter, the realization of a journey which they have already taken many times in their imagination ... Their years of fascination with *Dracula* means that most *Dracula* fans have developed a deep familiarity, not only with the story and its characters, but also with the landscape associated with the story. (2011: 238)

The in-depth description of Whitby by Stoker helps to create a foundation for a more enveloping intimacy for the pilgrim; seeing the spaces in real life which have only been experienced via media – films, books, and popular culture – transforms *Dracula* from myth to a possibility. This can aide in explaining the importance placed by the pilgrim of journeying to the far-flung locales described in the book; Reijnders also comments on the relationship between realistic and real, as 'by setting *Dracula* in a believable environment, Stoker hoped to give the supernatural events in the story a degree of believability' (ibid.). As Harry Potter's Platform 9 3/4 moves from fictional to actual, the landscape of Whitby allows for the possibility 'that perhaps *Dracula* was more than just imagination' (ibid.); because there was a 'real' physical place, it makes for a stronger possibility that other formerly imagined entities could also be true. Reijnders notes how this transitional state, between virtual and actual, is crucial, as it not only allows and encourages readers to become further invested in the book, it makes *Dracula*, though completely fantastical, anchored in the conceivable. The stairs, the graves, the church, the crumbling Abbey, the breathtaking views over the hills onto Whitby harbor – they are all real, just as Stoker portrayed them. Reijnders notes, 'this topographical realism provides a completely different advantage: the original novel and the later film versions provide numerous references that help the tourist identify Dracula Country' (2011: 239). This is crucial for continued investment and belief in the text as it is 'precisely these kinds of concrete objects and buildings [that] can develop into tactile references to an imagined universe' (238).

Fans who Reijnders interviewed during the course of his research underscore this theme between intellectual enrichment and spiritual enlightenment as provided by the media pilgrimage. He found that

> many [visitors] emphasized that they traveled to Whitby or Transylvania with the intention of deepening their emotional connection with the story ... respondents described how they would continually shift from a rational investigation of the environment to a more emotional, affective stance. (2011: 242)

It is essential to note here the break between the described 'rational' and 'emotional': these terms are not often challenged in the western world's acceptance of religion and theological ideals – which can easily be picked apart as just as transparent and flimsy, perhaps even more so, than the physicality offered in literary tourism. Yet the justification of the pilgrim to separate and explain what could be perceived as their 'irrational' importance and belief in the spaces and ideas offered up by the book points to both the media-induced secular journey to be still not accepted necessarily in the same manner as more traditional religious contexts while it simultaneously fulfills the same purpose. Reijnders's respondents talked about how their trips to Dracula country had allowed them to 'come "closer" to the story' and 'how being at the location gave them the feeling that they were making a "connection"' (2011: 242). What are they getting closer to, what are they wanting to connect to? The feeling of higher power, something ethereal, something non-tactile – the very traits associated with holy spaces.

LAST NIGHT I DREAMT I WENT TO MANDERLEY AGAIN

Daphne du Maurier's most popular novel, originally published in 1938, opens with this memorable line. Set in Cornwall on the fictional estate of Manderley, *Rebecca* combines murder, mystery, and jealousy, all told from the perspective of an unnamed narrator (only referred to throughout the text as Mrs. de Winter or the second Mrs. de Winter) as she reminisces about her past. Since its release, *Rebecca* has sold millions of copies, never been out of print, and has been adapted into plays, movies, television shows, and even an opera. Though she was raised in London, as an adult du Maurier lived and wrote in Cornwall, setting many of her novels in the coastal county, including *The Loving Spirit* (1931),[1] *Jamaica Inn* (1936), and *Frenchman's Creek* (1941). This created a permanent connection between author and region. Fans of her books have been making literary pilgrimages to the area du Maurier made famous for more than 80 years. Such trips are important as they further create a shared dialogue among readers, as 'the activity is not simply a function of "literary" influences ... it is a medium through which a range of cultural meaning and values may be communicated' (Squire, 1994: 104). Herbert further notes that

> The idea of literary pilgrims has existed for some time. It engenders the image of the dedicated scholar prepared to travel long distances to experience places linked with writers of prose, drama, or poetry, including the cemetery in Rome where the remains of Keats and Shelley lie. (2001: 312–3)

A du Maurier pilgrimage suggests similar commitment, as any reader familiar with her books will know. Her descriptions of Cornwall are in turn barren, wild, lush, untamed, and a bit scary: it is a landscape where anything may happen. Herbert argues that 'for most visitors, the word of the novel is more pervasive than the world of the writer' (1996: 77–85). However, both du Maurier and the Brontë sisters (who will be shortly discussed) have become intertwined with the settings of their books, as the 'pervasiveness' of space plays a crucial role in not only supplying inspiration for the writer but in perpetuating the myths surrounding the authors. Similar to the *Dracula* fan, du Maurier devout are looking for the same places which are described in the books; yet it is also the writer who is being fetishized, as the locations and sites which she once inhabited are being canonized in a religious fashion. In this way, du Maurier herself becomes

---

[1] In a sort of symbolic pilgrimage, the name of du Maurier's first book is based on a poem by Emily Brontë.

a draw to the area – not simply for her masterpieces, but almost as a desolate character and part of the narrative, blurring the definitions between fictional creations and the woman behind them.

In her work on Beatrix Potter, Squire argues that Potter's texts connect with one's own past and create identity, providing 'notions of heritage and a real past' that are often 'merged into overarching notions of "Englishness" and English heritage' (1996a: 83). They also allow fans the chance to further evaluate the importance of Potter's writing in their lives, as travel to such places provides room for 'scrutinizing ... relationships between texts and readers and the cultural meaning and values that may accrue to a literary oeuvre' (82). However, this can become problematic as this new simulacra is 'constantly juxtaposed against the urban present', as the ideals celebrated are 'a large part a product

Figure 14   One of many books connecting Daphne du Maurier with Cornwall; author's own. Photo: Jennifer Otter Bickerdike (2015)

of the urban imagination' (ibid.). The same argument can be applied to the modern presence of du Maurier in Cornwall. On one hand, as the visitor enters 'du Maurier Country' – the places associated with the author and her books – they appear at first glance to be unchanged since the author's death almost 30 years ago.

This is crucial for a positive pilgrimage experience, as Squire found in another study she did on tourism based on the *Anne of Green Gables* series. Her research (1996b) confirmed that the authenticity of a place and its 'historical accuracy' to what is written in the texts (though fictional) is perceived to be very important to the fan. Squire also found that '"authentic" heritage space has become a somewhat abstract concept' as 'much of this tourist development does not mirror literary heritage, literary images have shaped visitors impressions of place and serve as currency for a range of tourist sites, attractions, and promotional activities' (1996b: 126). The differentiation between real – what actually took place at a specific site – and the imagined – what occurred in an invented story, the thoughts, and feelings projected onto place by a reader – appear to be not important, as long as the allusion of legitimacy is employed, upheld, and evolved. Plate (2006: 104) writes of a bust in Bloomsbury of Virginia Woolf:

> By making the spot as the place where Woolf's literary work originated, linking the place to her literary production (rather than her life) – and doing so doubly, first by saying that Woolf lived, wrote and published nearby, then evoking walking round the square as her source and site of inspiration – [Woolf is memorialized] explicitly as a writer, attaching her texts, productivity and artistic person to a material site invested with symbolic meaning.

For du Maurier, the 'spots' are 'invested with symbolic meaning' not only because they were 'sites of inspiration' but also because the author has become so intertwined with the place that one seems to describe the other. In life, du Maurier was passionate and dedicated to her writing, often legendarily at the expense of being what biographers have referred to as 'aloof' from her husband and children. After her death, accusations that du Maurier had been bisexual further added to her renown as being in turn secretive, elusive, intense, and wild – reflecting the very attributes she described applying to Cornwall. This combination of contrasting meanings for both place and author dovetails with the push/pull of real and imagined experienced by the pilgrim. Visits to specific locations allow for a fan to feel almost as if they are metamorphosing into the icon, as the 'physical experience of space and place ... the sensory stimuli ... allow one to see what she [du Maurier] saw, but equally to hear, sense, and smell what she heard, sensed and smelled' (Plate, 2006: 107). Jeanette Winterson, who wrote about a visit to Virginia Woolf's home in Rodmell, Sussex, underscores this role-playing, as she 'encourages the literary pilgrim "to go and stand in the garden and look at the view. To see what she saw". As she [Winterson] says: "If you concentrate ... gradually the present will fade and the day trippers will fade so that the perspective becomes Virginia Woolf's"' (ibid.) – or, for the purpose here, Daphne du Maurier's.

Du Maurier's success during the years she lived in the southwest of England perpetuates this ideal of environment as stimulus, as many of the landmarks – whether located on the desolate moors, such as the Jamaica Inn, or the writer's own former home of Ferryside, located in Fowey – provide an unblemished setting, allowing the visitor to feel transported back a century, to when du Maurier first began visiting Cornwall on family trips. Busby and Hambly point out that although 'other authors had used Cornish locations in their plots', du Maurier was 'the first to attract significant popularity' (2000: 199–200). This was especially pertinent as she 'was writing at a time when conversion to the big screen first became a serious possibility' (ibid.) – thus opening up not only financial possibility but an array of mediums and outlets to showcase Cornwall. This conjunction is strengthened and buttressed constantly via books, travel brochures, and signs throughout the region alerting visitors who have entered 'du Maurier Country'.

Several entities have used the continued popularity of du Maurier to create attractions (e.g. commerce) into the region, with varying results. The annual Fowey Festival of Words and Music seeks to capitalize on the connection between the writer and Fowey, the location of her last residence in Cornwall. Originally called the 'du Maurier Festival', the event went through a name change in 2012 in an attempt to 'attract a new audience and a more diverse audience' (BBC. co.uk, 2012). This statement echoes the phenomena I experienced at the Jim Morrison grave – his name is more well known, but completely diluted of mean- ing. A spokesperson from the festival said that there had been questioning if 'whether the brand [of du Maurier] really was conveying the product [Cornwall? the festival?]' (ibid.). While there will still be a 'du Maurier content for the fans', the new evocation of the Fowey Festival of Words and Music will 'hopefully attract a wider and younger audience' (ibid.). This could prove to be detrimental to the lasting positive legacy of the writer on the region. Squire found in her work on Green Gables that there was a great concern from both the devout fan com- munity and the local residents of Prince Edward Island – where the Green Gables books are set – as to the massive departure from celebrating real author L.M. Montgomery to enhancing and focusing on the fictional time/place described in the books. Squire noted that there were 'concerns about excessive commercialism

of literary heritage expresse[d] regularly ... one observer commented, It's surprising ... Montgomery's headstone hasn't become a whirling dervish from her
turning over in her grave' (1996b: 124). Busby and Hambly found similar concerns in their study of du Maurier country, as 'When an area becomes affected
by mass tourism, a sense of resentment can be felt by local residents; this equally
applies to development based on literary association which would normally be
expected to attract lower numbers' (2000: 205). In regard to the festival in
Fowey, Busby and Hambly found that 'those living in the area for more than
33 years (the population is predominantly aged over 45) tended to perceive the
festival as a negative; clearly there is not a case of recently-retired-in-migrants
who do not want the Festival in their "backyard"' (208). The town needs the
visitors; located in the same county as Port Isaac of *Doc Martin* fame, Fowey suf-
fers from many of the very financial predicaments that such tourist-dependent
communities have in common. Andrew (1997) notes the possible benefits of
expanding the event to be more inclusive and less focused on du Maurier, as 'if
the indigenous industries are naturally in decline, tourism can offer a replacement for them'. However, the very inspiration for the festival – du Maurier – is
all but erased as the new breed of festival goers are more likely to be tourists,
not fans. Busby and Hambly concur, as this influx of 'visitors are unlikely to bring
high levels of literary awareness with them and they would appear to be moti-
vated more by the simple entertainment value of the Festival – if the small survey
is taken to be representative' (2000: 209) – thus erasing the original meaning
and spirit of the event.

MEMORIAL ROOM

Du Maurier found inspiration upon the moors of Bodmin for her 1936 novel
Jamaica Inn. Folklore has it that while out horse riding in the area, the author
became enveloped in a foggy mist and disoriented. Her mount somehow made
it back to the Jamaica Inn, where du Maurier stayed for several days, recovering
from the ordeal. During her time there, she soaked up the wind-swept and desolate atmosphere and heard many stories about the pirates and smuggling which
had once taken place under the very same roof. She used these tales as plot points
and the dreary location as the setting for her famous novel of the same name.

The Inn has taken it upon itself to create a 'Memorial Room' to the author
on its premises. In its defense, there does not exist any other center or fully
envisioned du Maurier museum. The du Maurier Literary Centre in Fowey is
basically a book store comprised of some large panels describing the connection between the town and the author. The Fowey Museum itself is very small

and encompasses the history of the village, hence not exclusive to du Maurier. Thus there is a need and space in the county for a proper homage and celebration of the author. Sadly, the Jamaica Inn is not that.

From the outside, the Jamaica Inn looks as dismal as du Maurier described it. According to du Maurier biographer Hilary Macaskill (2013), 'Daphne lamented in later life that she had given it [The Jamaica Inn] such tourism potential: "As a motorist, I pass by with some embarrassment, feeling myself to blame"'. Macaskill reports of her own pilgrimage to the Inn, 'We didn't stop. It might have spoiled the magic' (ibid.). At first glance, Bodmin seems identical to the du Maurier depiction. Barren moors stretch far into the horizon. The concrete patio frontage does not entice one to get out of the car and explore what other delights may await inside the inn-cum-restaurant. Once inside, the visitor is besieged by an all-encompassing dour, rundown vibe, reminiscent of a moldy amusement park pub, the stale smell of old shoes and ancient deep-fried food hanging heavy in the air. It was clear how such a setting could inspire the depressive tone of the du Maurier novel, though perhaps more for the shabby griminess of the Inn than for fanciful fables of past glories. It seemed more haunted by outdated decor, peeling wallpaper, and poor ventilation – a possibly scarier set of specters – than the ghosts of various smugglers who are said to roam the premises.

The Inn boasts of having the du Maurier Memorial Room 'full of memorabilia'. However, after stripping the pilgrim of the £4 entry fee, it becomes apparent that the description of 'room' is overly generous – though the use of 'memorial' is accurate – the space does indeed have the somber atmosphere one may find at a funeral parlor. The homage consists of a dusty-looking desk at which the author supposedly once sat at, along with an overflowing ashtray of half-smoked cigarettes, a typewriter, and some 'casually' tossed paperbacks of her various books (because all scribes surround themselves with numerous copies of their own work while writing). It almost feels a bit insulting to both writer and fan, as the former is not so much celebrated as exploited, as the 'Room' also features one of the largest gift shops ever attached to a rundown pub – while the latter leaves feeling cheated and let down – the opposite emotion that du Maurier evoked in her canonizing of the region.

TAKE ME TO MENABILLY

In a vein reminiscent of Dracula Castle, Manderley as described in *Rebecca* only exists within the pages of the book. However, legend has it that du Maurier based the imaginary estate on the real Menabilly, the home that the writer eventually leased for over 20 years. Like Bran being envisioned into Dracula castle,

Menabilly allows the pilgrim to have a focal point in the physical with which to navigate the text. The estate is still privately owned, allowing the reader to further project Manderley onto Menabilly. However, two smaller properties on the estate are available as vacation rentals – the Keepers Cottage and the Polridmouth Cottage. These provide the fan with a similar experience to that described by the unnamed protagonist in *Rebecca* – the visitor is at once of the space, as they are occupying the same place as Menabilly – yet they are simultaneously cut off from the seeming authentic by not staying in or viewing the inner workings of the actual house, much as the second Mrs. de Winter is shut out for most of the book from the truth about her surroundings. The irony here is that the 'real' Manderley has never existed. Yet the pilgrim needs to find relation between text and actual location. In her research on *Anne of Green Gables*, Squire found that though 'neither landscapes nor literature are fixed entities and, in her writings, Montgomery depicted a mythical golden age that never really existed, much regional tourist development has been pre-mised upon idealized images of late 19th-century rural society' (1996b: 129); a similar phenomenon is arguably in play at Menabilly. The fantasy of Manderley as described by and inhabited in *Rebecca* could easily be broken if the pilgrim were to actually tour the premises. The inaccessibility of the place allows for the fictional depiction to become the real, Menabilly to be Manderley.

Such separation has proved to be equally important in maintaining the mag-ical aura of Ferryside, the property in Fowey that du Maurier's parents bought one year while on a holiday. It is here that a young Daphne did much of her early work. The du Maurier family still lives in the house, which is not accessible to the public. The pilgrim has to be satisfied with the view of the exterior facade, offered either while adrift on the Fowey River Estuary or from above while sitting on a balcony at the nearby Old Ferry Inn. Here the second Mrs. de Winter's trials and tribulations are again felt, as the visitor is denied access to the insider experience of the house, having to be satisfied with glimpses secretly stolen from afar. 'Du Maurier County' may exist only as a state of mind, as for even the most dedicated pilgrim, space and place are only truly authentic in evoking the moods and emotions of the author's work, especially that of inaccessibility.

HAWORTH AND THE BRONTË MYTH

Out on the wiley, windy moors

We'd roll and fall in green.

You had a temper like my jealousy:

Too hot, too greedy.

How could you leave me,

When I needed to possess you?

I hated you. I loved you, too.

('Wuthering Heights', Kate Bush)

Bush's 1978 anthem conjures up in these few lines, the emotive nature of the land-scapes and characters created in Emily Brontë's book of the same name. The song is an example of how iconic the novel, the writers, and even the title have become in popular rhetoric. The Brontë sisters are intrinsically and irrevocably the unique selling point for not only the quaint northern village of Haworth, where they spent much of their lives, but for the entire surrounding area, which is referred to not by individual town names but simply as 'Brontë Country'. Similar to Cornwall, the entire region financially depends on the continuous renewal of the Brontë myth to bring visitors and commerce to the area. While du Maurier is arguably one component in attracting tourists to the county where she lived and set her stories, the Brontës *are* the industry. The myth of the three writer sisters has become bigger and arguably more important in the material of culture than the very books they wrote. They are now almost interchangeable with the characters in their novels, as pilgrims come to search for not only what inspired them but what it was like to *be* them: female authors in a male-dominated literary world, brought up in a harsh, barren setting, with little connection to the 'outside' (read: sophisticated) world. Simon Goldhill underscores this point, adding, '*Wuthering Heights* ... has become the sort of cultural icon that means that you recognize the atmosphere even if you don't remember the plot [of the book]' (2011: 61). Plate's work further supports this idea:

> writers are remembered by tracing their (or their characters) steps through the spaces described in their books, their names evoked to attach to place, their memory celebrated in rituals that involve complex engagements between local inhabitants and tourists in transit, 'city branding' and the marketing of space as 'cultural capital' in both senses of the term. (2006: 102)

The potent pairing of dramatic, gothic narrative with the portrayal of the trio as sheltered, tragic figures creates a myriad of questions relating not necessar-ily to the works themselves but places the interest on the women who wrote them. How could these country mice girls write such compelling stories of intrigue, desire, and hardship? To visit 'Brontë Country' is to search for this information first-hand; however, the pilgrimage also reveals a theme found in the other case studies of literary pilgrimage – fiction usurping fact in the face of providing and evolving the continued legends and beliefs in the myths.

Credit for much of the founding ideas about the sisters and 'Brontë Country' can be attributed to Elizabeth Gaskell. Gaskell released her biography about Charlotte in 1857, two years after the authoress had passed away. Gaskell based much of the book on correspondence sent by Charlotte to close friend Ellen Nussey. Gaskell deliberately left out crucial information about the writer's life and pumped up the dramatic effect of other aspects. Her depictions of Haworth, the Brontë family, and the constant adversity faced by the sisters aided in creating the current framework for the myth of the Brontës. Gaskell's depiction, though not necessarily based on exact fact, became the story of famous writers, as

> its [the books'] fame came mostly from its vivid and compelling picture of a poor family in a remote village discovering their own literary talent and cautiously bringing it before an amazed world … It was Mrs. Gaskell who made Haworth the key to the Brontë life, who painted the picture of the pure, thoroughly coarse sites, loving the moors, tending their father and brother, producing great art in humble Yorkshire. (Goldhill, 2011: 63–4)

Figure 15   Moors of 'Brontë Country', Haworth, England. Photo: Jennifer Otter Bickerdike (2013)

As the pilgrim ascends into the hilly Brontë country, they are immediately thrust into the setting of any book written by the trio – but more poignantly, thrust into Gaskell's description of the Brontë's native surroundings. In the Brontë books, the landscapes jump off the page as being simultaneously claustrophobic in their lack of brightness, yet endless, large, and empty – a characteristic which Gaskell expands upon in her biography on Charlotte.

Figure 16 What authoress does not dream of being featured on a tea towel? Author's own. Photo: Jennifer Otter Bickerdike (2015)

Goldhill notes (2011: 65), 'the physical surroundings are made to take on all the oppressiveness of a tragic life'. Mrs. Gaskell quotes from a friend's pilgrimage to Haworth:

> The country got wilder and wilder and wilder as we approached Haworth; for the last four miles we were ascending a huge moor, at the very top of which lies the dreary black-looking village of Haworth … a dreary, dreary place literally *paved* [authors italics] with rain blackened tombstones … There was an old man in the churchyard, brooding like a Ghoul over the graves, with a sort of grim hilarity on his face. I thought he looked hardly human; however, he was human enough to tell us the way. (Ibid.)

Gaskell's depiction in affect *tells* the visitor the way – the manner by which to frame not only the stories written by the Brontës but the story *of* the Brontës: a haunted landscape, thick with depressive grey and lacking any opportunity of escape. Gaskell's Haworth, according to Goldhill, 'prepare[s] [any visitor to Haworth] for the sisters' life as suffering artists' (ibid.). Depending on the time of year, the hills of the moors comprising 'Brontë Country' are either green, yellow, and lavender with rolling grasses, or burnt, barren brown; they seem to stretch endlessly across and over the horizon. The sky is unique in that it reflects the same vastness, the same empty, never-ending spectrum. Sheep dot the hillsides. Barriers in this area are stone walls, constructed with overlapping rocks. Upon arrival, the pilgrim must walk further up into Haworth proper, along a cobbled, narrow, twisting road. Shops line the streets, most adorned with names reflecting the inescapable tie between the family and the village: Brontë Vintage Crockery, Brontë Hotel, Charlotte's Tea Room. The connection is further strengthened by the vast array of Brontë-themed items for sale, from tea towels to toilet roll.

A red phone box looks incredibly vulgar and out of place, as all of the buildings are made from similar stone materials as comprise the various farm walls.

The overriding color scheme is old grey and depressive brown. The lack of modernity adds to the effect of 19th-century slumming, as the village appears to have been perfectly preserved since the Brontë's time. Arguably, the presented Haworth has been molded to fit and support the Brontë myth, one of deprivation, death, and despair. The story of Charlotte Brontë in particular has become one of feminist trial,

> the story of the girl who struggled to find a voice, who epitomizes the difficulties of becoming a writer as a woman, then of course, but still now. Haworth stands for every woman's home, the repression of inner self in spacial propriety – and Charlotte's need to use a man's name to publish at first demonstrates the social

constraints against which she fights, just as *Jane Eyre* is the story of a girl's journey into self-assertion, a pilgrimage in itself. Haworth is the symbol of a woman's
struggle for self-expression. (Goldhill, 2011: 68)

Notice here that Goldhill connects Charlotte with not only the trials of female
writers but with the very character she created and the village where she lived,
forming an equation of equality among the four. To live with such strife, then die
at a young age has become an integral part of the myth, not only for Charlotte
but for 'the fate of the woman writer' (Watson, 2006: 38–9). It is imperative,
therefore, that Haworth properly reflects the myth, so as to not only uphold but
evolve the Brontë (and arguably the tragic woman writer) ideal. Watson notes,

> Haworth was made into the likeness of the Brontës ... and so betrays more
> explicit[ly] what the culture wished to make of the sisters ... Haworth drama-
> tizes female authorship as unsuccessful to the point of invisibility ... Haworth
> provides a dysphoric, not to say Gothic, narrative of female repression, suffering
> and death ... Haworth is designed principally as a memorial to dead young
> women ... Haworth presents a diffusion, a portability, a perishability of sites of
> writing both within the house and out on the moors. (2006: 92).

Figure 17 Depressive tones in Haworth, England. Photo: Jennifer Otter Bickerdike (2013)

The 'invisibility' that Watson describes is the vanishing of the sisters, perhaps even symbolic of women authoresses, into the myth, as embedded as
part and parcel of Haworth: not viewed as individuals, incapable of existing
outside of the context of the Victorian stone buildings. On her own literary
pilgrimage to Haworth, Virginia Woolf said, 'Haworth and the Brontës are
somehow inextricably mixed. It expresses the Brontës, the Brontës express
it; they fit like a snail its shell' (1980 [1904]). This is no accident, as Watson
purports,

> In the summer, it is hardly possible to move in the village streets for the throngs
> of local and foreign tourists "doing" Haworth ... this ... is because the Yorkshire
> Tourist Board has been aggressively and successfully embedding the parsonage
> within the granulized 'heritage' landscape compounded of the sublime discom-
> fort of the moors, obsolete industrialism and a shopping experience of rugs and
> fudge. (2006: 92)

Amidst the marketing and, more importantly, the belief that Haworth is of
upmost importance in the Brontë myth, it is crucial to remember, as Anderson
and Robinson point out, that 'Haworth itself ... features in none of the Brontës
novels. Its appeal is as the setting of the Brontës *lives*' (2002: 145). Haworth
has thus been formed to fit the financial and cultural expectations of Brontë.
This intermingling of truth and tale has had the affect of 'flattening out ...
the distinction between biographical and fictional, effectively locat[ing] the sisters [Brontë] in the same physical space and on the same imaginative plane
as [their] characters' (Watson, 2006: 123). These issues become increasingly
problematic as even the promotional materials for the region interchange the
women with the characters, 'encourag[ing] visitors to "see life through the
eyes of Charlotte Brontë's *Jane Eyre*: who stands in the winds which buffeted
Wuthering Heights and chased ghosts of Cathy and Heathcliff across the bluff,
bold swells of heath"' (Tetley, 1998: 14).

BRONTË PARSONAGE AND THE KNOWLEDGE OF KNICKERS

The Brontë Parsonage offers another example of how 'the boundaries between
fact and fiction, the real and the metaphorical ... [are becoming] increasingly
blurred and increasingly indistinct' (Tetley, 1998: 14). At first (and honestly
second and third) glance, the Parsonage looks exactly as the pilgrim would
expect it to. In 1820, Brontë patriarch Patrick was appointed to the Parsonage
in Haworth. It is here that the famous sisters spent most of their lives, wrote
their books, and found inspiration. After the success of *Jane Eyre*, fans began

flocking to Haworth to catch a glimpse of the authoress and cobble further meaning. Thus began the precarious balance between authenticity and presentation. Anderson and Robinson note,

> for the rest of [Charlotte's] life, visitors were to arrive in Haworth and knock at the Parsonage door, drawn there by the fame of her novels and the mystery of their authorship ... visitors were received with good grace, particularly if they were young aspiring authors. More often they aroused in this shy, intensely private person annoyance and panic. (2002: 143–4)

However, the full potential draw of the Parsonage was not realized until after Charlotte's death, with the writing of Gaskell's biography. Once the very human (thus flawed) sisters were gone, the myth could fully be realized, and the Parsonage's, and arguably Haworth's, fiscal possibilities could be truly exploited. Goldhill notes how,

> The Parsonage had become a shrine full of myths: the children making up stories, as the first steps of literary genius; the sisters caring for father in the parlor, the icon of duty; the sisters staring out of the window, quietly passionate. The house has been turned by all those biographers of the Brontës, all those films, all those parodies, from a place to which the family moved because the father got a job there, to a foundation of literary genius and feminine soul. (2011: 66)

The building looks out onto the village's cemetery, consisting of bleak, crowded, ancient graves literally on top of one another, overgrown with moss. Such a macabre and arguably creepy setting was daily life in the Brontë's time, as 'Death was all too insistently familiar to Haworth: over 41 percent of children died before they were six years old, and there are incredibly twenty thousand burials in what is a small, walled, cemetery. Old Patrick Brontë buried many hundreds of children apart from his own' (Goldhill, 2011: 76).

Though outdoors, the graveyard gives off a feeling of suffocation. Goldhill's dour description underscores this:

> There are no grass borders, no flowers, and the shadow from the trees and the black soil between the gray-green, weighty memorials, give the scene a darkness that was easy to imagine seeping into the Brontë's writing ... The church and the graveyard fill the view through the front windows of the parsonage, as the moors fill the back. (Ibid.)

Figure 18   The former Brontë home at the Parsonage in Haworth, overlooking the village's cemetery. Photo: Jennifer Otter Bickerdike (2013)

Watson concurs,

> the Parsonage looks satisfyingly like a setting for a Gothic novel, pressed behind by the wild high flat-backed moors and fronted by a churchyard heaving uncomfortably with blackened streaked gravestones – some flat, some upright, some broken and tilting as though the dead were forcing themselves up uneasily through sodden strips of grass – pressing hard up against the wall that divides the churchyard from the tiny garden. (2006: 107–8)

It was not until more than 60 years after the death of the last Brontë standing, father Patrick, that the Parsonage was purchased and transformed into a museum. Here lies one of the contradictions within the space: though it was originally purposed as an archive for all that is Brontë, most of the Parsonage is staged to appear as if the famous family will be returning to the rooms momentarily, thus precariously shifting from a family home to institution, from private to public. Goldhill concurs,

The parsonage tries to do two things at once. It wants to give a sense of the house as it was lived in: so we have the dining room with its books and a table with little objects from the sisters on it. 'This is where it all happened...' But it is also a museum. (2011: 73)

Upon entry, the visitor is immediately thrust into the main dining/family room of the writers, where various pieces of furniture formerly belonging to the Brontës are reverently displayed. This includes a table where *Wuthering Heights*, *Jane Eyre*, and *Agnes Grey* were written and the macabre addition of a black couch, legendarily the place where Emily Brontë died. Anderson and Robinson argue that the appeal of such items comes from the idea that such

> houses, apartments and rooms ... have borne witness to various stages of a writer's life from birth to death. Writer's homes as focal destinations provide tan-gible connections between the created and the creator ... for literary pilgrims ... here lies the potential for intimacy, authenticity ... the notion that the visitor is where the author's pen physically touched paper or his/her fingers the keys on the typewriter. (2002: 15)

There is no denying the physical, visceral reaction to such objects. It is almost impossible to ignore the overt need to lie upon the death couch, to some-how embody the author, crossing time and place for even a moment in an imaginary communion between visitor and long-departed Brontë. Anderson and Robinson argue that this appeal comes from the individualistic process of writing meeting the public space of readership, noting, 'The writing process is generally a solitary, staccato process ... to the outsider, the work and the spaces that work are imbued with mystique: here, in the writer's house, we are in the surroundings where that private process took place' (2002: 15–6). This connection between place, space, and material objects and the conflicting museum/home conundrum continues as the pilgrim works their way through the house. Most notable is the transformation of the mundane into the pre-cious. Dog collars, old shoes, and petticoats are protected under glass and soft lit; upon viewing Charlotte's bedroom, which is adorned with some of her clothes, including 'a rather faded cream stocking with a hole near the top of the thigh', Goldhill questions such fetishization, remarking, 'What Victorian woman, let alone the cripplingly shy Charlotte, would want her used under-wear on display?' (2011: 74). However, Anderson and Robinson view such commodity worship as 'central to the connectivity experienced by visitors', as such 'objects, artifacts of daily reality ... are conferred with hyper-significance and reverence' (2002: 17). Goldhill confronts this behavior, noting,

> The fascination with the Brontës bites deep and leads the biographer to walk in every footstep, to collect every discarded tchotchke as a relic (Anne's *teapot* [author's emphasis] is a 'silent witness' to her true character ...), and to believe that you can get to their inner world by living where they lived. The only other place you see language like this is with religious pilgrims. (2011: 71)

This relationship between myth, author, and reader has proved to be consistently profitable in the case of the Brontës, regardless of the questionable set-up. Anderson and Robinson concur,

> on their death, authors can become heroes, icons, focal points for generations and symbols for an age. This lends itself well to an industry that trades on symbols, icons and anniversaries, where writers do not really die, they just become more powerful brands. (2002: 19)

On a recent visit, a line of tourists, over 75 people deep, waited outside the Parsonage for the doors to open to the day's business.

Figure 19   Rain or shine, the devout line-up to visit the Brontë Parsonage, Haworth, England. Photo: Jennifer Otter Bickerdike (2013)

Figure 20   Japanese visitors soak up the Haworth atmosphere. Photo: Jennifer Otter Bickerdike (2013)

It was a cold November morning, yet another large group, mostly of Japanese college students, took pictures nearby. There is a slight drizzle; one of the students opened a 'Brontë' umbrella, emblazoned with portraits of the three sisters. The atmosphere is bleak as any scene from *Agnes Grey* – perfectly fulfilling the visitors' expectations for miserableness.

TOP WITHENS AND THE IMAGINED GRAVES

Besides Haworth and the Parsonage, two other spaces provide central meaning to the literary tourist in Brontë country. However, as found in the two other case studies, the places play a crucial role in upholding and aiding in the continued worth and belief in the Brontë myth, while concurrently having little to no basis in any real tie to the meaning they are adorned with. Imperative to any thorough Brontë pilgrimage is a trek up to Top Withens,[2]

---

[2]   There have historically been two contrasting spellings for the dilapidated farmhouse, Withens and Withins. Here Withens will be used throughout.

a former poultry farm which has been abandoned since 1926. Though there are 'no known records that state any reference of a Brontë connection to Top Withens, it has been passed down locally that the ruins are connected to Emily Brontë's novel *Wuthering Heights*' (haworth-village.org.uk). After a perilous near-three-mile hike through rough, uphill, often muddy terrain, those brave enough to conquer the trail are rewarded with the ruins of the estate – a small, stone house. The relationship between the derelict rubble and the Brontës is dubious at best, yet that did not stop the Brontë Society placing a plaque at the site in 1964 stating

> This farmhouse has been associated with 'Wuthering Heights', the Earnshaw home in Emily Brontë's novel. The buildings, even when complete, bore no resemblance to the house she described, but the situation may have been in her mind when she wrote of the moorland setting of the Heights. This plaque has been placed here in response to many enquiries. (Howarth Village, no date)

This convoluted statement both denies and strengthens the importance of Top Withens in the context of the Brontë myth: it simultaneously declares that there is 'no resemblance' between the beaten-up stones 'even when complete' with the *Wuthering Heights* described by Emily – thus admitting no authentic tie between the house and the Brontës. However, the plaque goes on to position this fabricated location as *the* location – a Haworthian Bran Castle – stating unequivocally that the farmhouse 'has been associated with' the famous novel and that the 'situation may have been in her [Emily's] mind', thus consecrating the place as important and valid – even though the former sentence does just the opposite. Top Withens as the home of *Wuthering Heights* is such an accepted part of the Brontë myth worldwide that signs leading up to it are in several languages, including Japanese. This illustrates what Goldhill claims is 'the creation of the image ... trump[ing] the reality' (2011: 65).

However, perhaps strangest of all is the actual final resting places of the Brontë sisters. Anderson and Robinson (2002: 19) argue that 'Dead authors ... provide us with graves and memorials to visit ... tangible signatures of a writer's presence, and commonly accessible to the public'. To conclude a pilgrimage with a visit to the grave of the icons is to allow for a

> sense of mourning like that felt by one friend for another ... [and] demands that the dead be located, and a sense that at the graves that historical event [which made the icon famous] is, uniquely still acting, still contemporary: "the dust that covered by his tomb, is simply and *literally the great man himself*". (Godwin, 1809: 20)

Watson underscores this, as 'the grave is not merely a grave it is a home ... which as far as they are at all on the earth, *they still inhabit'* (2006: 35–6). The grave offers further intimacy to the pilgrim as it is unique. Watson argues that

> the grave of an author could be considered anti-book in the extreme. Whereas a book is by definition mass-produced for while the text of a book is printed, the text of a tomb is inscribed and engraven ... One is impersonal and promiscuous, the other personalized and faithfully authorized. (2006: 38)

Here lies another massive rupture between the Brontë myth and the actual truth. Though almost the entire mystique of the sisters is based upon place (Haworth) and the interchangeable nature between their characters and their lives, the Brontës are not buried in the Haworth cemetery. Watson contends that there is an expectation for the sisters to have been buried within the grave-yard: the very place, in life, that they looked out upon from their windows day in and out – thus adding to the macabre, tragic legend of fated finality. This assumption has been 'derived from the fate of Catherine Earnshaw [protag-onist of Emily's *Wuthering Heights*] who is, at her own request, buried in the open at ... the churchyard in *Wuthering Heights* rather than inside the church' (Watson, 2006: 111). Charlotte and Emily's remains are interred in a vault out of view within St. Michael's, the Haworth church over which her father pro-ceeded. Anne Brontë is buried by herself in Scarborough, almost 100 miles from Haworth. The reality of 'the Brontës respectable, middle class female family life, which mandated family burial in the church crypt, is over-written for tourist-readers by the romantic location Emily invented for her heroines grave' (ibid.). The actual sites of the tombs, specifically that of Charlotte, have almost been forgotten and erased through the displacement of the women for the characters they wrote. Popular culture has placed their graves as out-side, thus allowing for them to be 'strew with roses the grave' (Arnold, 1855) and 'all overgrown with tuning moss' (Dickinson, no date). A plaque in the church graveyard 'tacitly acknowledge[s] th[e] fruitless hunt that many have made amongst the gravestones [looking for the sisters] before discovering the memorial inside the church' (Watson, 2006: 110). It is almost surprising that the remains have not been moved to a location that dovetails more neatly with the fictional books, allowing for even further emergence between fact and imaginary.

CONCLUSION: THE MIGHTY HORDES

Recently my husband and I attended a wedding in Brighton, England. Brighton is a seaside city, vibrant, sparkly, and filled with independent shops, cafes, restaurants, and a lively culture scene. It is famously the location for the Who's epic 1979 movie *Quadrophenia*. We had arrived for the nuptials midmorning and been inside the church for several hours. Upon emerging into the early-afternoon sunlight, we were directed to travel about half a mile, easily walkable, to where the reception and wedding breakfast were taking place.

We had only gone about ten steps when a major road block asserted itself – a swarm of zombies. Many had elaborate makeup, with fake lesions, cuts, and gore erupting from faces, hands, and necks, stained and raggedy clothes adorning shuffling participants and a muddled cacophony of grunts and groans intermittently emerging from the hundred-or-so strong in front of us. Having been shielded by the early start time of the event and the tucked-away nature of the church, unbeknown to us there was a 5-k run with a zombie theme going on at the same time as our friends' ceremony. 'Run' is probably a generous word, as many of the participants had also appropriated the popular lurch of the undead, often accented by dragging feet or awkwardly held hands. We ducked into a pub, in an attempt to wait them out. However, apparently zombies also hanker for a pint, as the establishment was filled with revelers who seemed more keen on imbibing a brew than finishing the three miles of the 'run'.

Brighton is not alone in hosting such events. A quick search online reveals countless such experiences on offer, ranging from simply dressing up as your favorite rendition of brain eater and trotting along a planned course (and occasionally stopping along the way for a beer) to participants being chased by hordes of the undead across a lengthy course, to strategic 'zombie evacuations', where people pay to be attacked by zombies. If you cannot get to Atlanta to see, feel, and touch the actual spaces profiled in

The Walking Dead, the popularity and ubiquitous nature of such happenings arguably illustrates a similar longing to be, to step in to, at least for the several hours of the events, the monstrous horror featured on the show. It is creating or attempting to mimic the scenes from the television on the familiar streets, a merging of the symbolic pilgrimage – taking elements from the mediatized entity – and making the everyday momentarily spectacular and transformed into a place of importance, enacting Atlanta in the roads of one's own town, if even for a day.

The various zombie runs illustrate a need to escape the daily grind through creating a fantastical, though momentary, universe of the undead, in essence making a symbolic pilgrimage to *The Walking Dead* by transplanting the television show onto one's available locality. The zombie runners transpose Atlanta onto any nearby, accessible cityscape – in a way, taking the nondescript feature of *The Walking Dead*'s southern setting as applicable to any town – whether idyllic Brighton or any of the various staging sites in Australia, China, or Singapore for the roving Run For Your Lives happenings – events billed as 'one part obstacle course, one part music festival, one part escaping the clutches of zombies – and all parts awesome' (YouTube, 2015).

The MozArmy attempts to create a similarly imaginary world, perpetuating a mythical moment of faux nostalgia. The 'MozArmy' is a group of 'Loyal fans of Morrissey, his band, and his work with The Smiths' (Facebook, 2015). The gathering, held at the Star and Garter, a venue well known in fan circles for hosting a long-running monthly Morrissey/Smiths disco, boasted panel discussions on the lead singer, Morrissey-inspired shopping, vegan food, and a 'three-hour tour taking fans to Kings Road, Salford Lads Club, The Iron Bridge and many more Smiths haunts', encouraging fans to 'Make [their] pilgrimage!' on the specially-kitted-out 'Mozbus' (Morrissey-solo, 2013). MozArmy stages its get-togethers in the mythical musical stronghold of Manchester, as its unique characteristics and description are instilled in many of the songs and more so the mystique shrouding The Smiths and Morrissey. As the purposeful interchangeability of *The Walking Dead* allows for any town to become *The Walking Dead*, Manchester alone plays a crucial part in the make-up of the Morrissey brand – a backdrop of deprivation, red brick buildings, 'a river the color of lead',[1] grey skies, Whalley Range.[2] To fully understand The Smiths – therefore, to fully engage with an individual's quest for personal identity and relationship as provided by the band – one has to see and

---

[1] Lyric from The Smiths 1983 song, 'This Night Has Opened My Eyes'.

[2] Lyric from The Smiths 1984 song, 'Miserable Lie'.

experience the places that created the myth, personally trot the 'side-streets that you slip down'.[3] By normalizing, even strongly encouraging such pilgrimage, the MozArmy Meet Up creates a temporary universe for its participants, underscoring the importance of such journeys as a means to fully embrace the music of the band as messianic, the spaces as holy.

There is something romantic and unarguably appealing about seeing first-hand the places that have only been experienced through the two-dimensional movie or TV screen, imagined via songs or books. The charge of tracing a personal icon's footsteps gives the participant at once a feeling of communion with the mediated figure not often available or achievable in daily life, while also allowing for a momentary glimpse at possible brilliance – of one's own ability to create and necessitate cultural movement in a similar manner. In his book *The Dylanologists: Adventures in the Land of Bob*, David Kinney profiles several fans of Bob Dylan who illustrate this precarious tight rope between protecting valuable assets for future generations to admire and possibly be inspired by and the questionable obsession with such figures and spaces asso-ciated with them (recalling the addition of Charlotte Brontë's undies on display at the Parsonage in Haworth). Upon arriving in Dylan's hometown of Hibbing, Minnesota, Kinney (2014) finds that the pilgrim 'could see the coffee shop where he [Dylan] ate cherry pie with his girlfriend' – in fact, the fan could even eat their own cherry pie in the same shop, an experience which was described by one visitor as her 'idea of heaven' (ibid.).

Kinney goes on to profile one devotee, Bill Pagel, who has spent over 20 years dedicated to creating an archive of all things Dylan related. His collec-tion includes telephone directories from the years that the folk singer's family lived in Hibbing, high school yearbooks featuring Bob signatures, and 'a ceramic candy bowl that once belonged to Dylan's grandmother. It sat on a faux-gold stand, and guitar strumming dandies serenaded fair maidens on the cracked lid, which was messily glued back together after, Bill was told, Bob busted it' (ibid.). Pagel's collection has grown so vast that 'he was not able to physically fit all of [it] … in his house, [and has] rented climate-controlled storage units for the overflow' (ibid.).

However, Pagel's most expensive purchase is arguably the house where the singer was born in 1941. Pagel is attempting to rebuild it to exactly resemble its appearance when the Zimmerman[4] family lived there. No detail is too small,

---

[3]   Lyric from The Smiths 1988 song, 'Panic'.

[4]   Bob Dylan's real last name.

as Pagel is 'relying on photographs unearthed from the 1940s for accuracy' and 'for precision's sake, he counted each wooden tine in the photos' (ibid.). Kinney notes how 'even in Dylan circles, Bill's peculiar collection was regarded with awe, and some alarm' (ibid.). Yet he also points out, 'Bill said he was not obsessed but *dedicated* [Kinney's emphasis]. He was an archivist, a preservationist and he was driven to save all this material for later generations' (ibid.).

After Pagel purchases the high chair from which baby Bob was fed, Kinney asks, 'Would it cross some kind of weirdness Rubicon to own this piece? What would another Bob Dylan collector do? What if it were, say, Shakespeare's? Wouldn't a museum curator snap *that* [Kinney's emphasis] up in a second?' (ibid.). Here is crux of secular belief – if said high chair had once held a baby Jesus, a baby Muhammad, hell, a baby John Lennon, would it not hold the same pride of place and importance in the cultural context of sacred items? Pagel's collection may appear creepy, as Dylan is (of this writing) still a living, breathing, somewhat contemporary figure, in contrast to one lost in the cerements of history and myth. However, *the very same* behavior is exhibited by the millions of pilgrims at the Shroud of Turin, or those who come to lay eyes on the box said to contain hair follicles once belonging to the beard of the prophet Muhammad. Scholars on Christianity believe that only three or four nails were actually used to crucify Christ; yet more than 40 such relics have claimed to be authentic and 'found' throughout the last two thousand years. If religious traditions are momentarily put to the side, how different is comparing a piece of cloth to a piece of hair to a signature in a yearbook to a rotten tooth[5]? It is the belief and the worth projected onto each item which makes it important, just as the most mundane space has been turned holy and sacred via similar shared meaning. The surge in technology has allowed such various convictions to quickly be spread, contemplated, and normalized in a way never previously experienced in history. It is reverential for a Morrissey fan to walk the streets of Manchester, to write their own message on the walls of the Iron Bridge – *I was here. I am part of the story. I am of this.*

The secular activity of pilgrimage illustrates the religious attributes provided by such actions. When a television show, a book, or a 'song can save your life',[6] perhaps it is the mediated entity that is the light that never goes out[7] in our current technology-driven world.

---

[5] A rotten tooth which had been removed from the Beatles' John Lennon was auctioned off for nearly £20,000 in 2013.

[6] Lyric from The Smiths 1986 song, 'The Queen Is Dead'.

[7] Lyric from The Smiths 1986 song, 'There Is a Light That Never Goes Out'.

Figure 21   The Iron Bridge, Manchester, England, as described in The Smiths 1984 song, 'Still Ill'. Photo: Jennifer Otter Bickerdike (2008)

Figure 22   I was here. Graffiti on the Iron Bridge. Photo: Jennifer Otter Bickerdike (2008)

REFERENCES

24 Hour Party People (2002) Dir. Michael Winterbottom. Revolution Films.

Anderson, H.C. & Robinson, M. (2002) *Literature and Tourism: Reading and Writing Tourism Texts*. Edited by H.C. Anderson & M. Robinson. London & New York: Continuum.

Andrew, B.P. (1997) 'Tourism and the Economic Development of Cornwall'. In *Annals of Tourism Research*, Vol. 24 (3), 721–735.

Arnold, M. (1855) 'Haworth Churchyard'. Available at http://www.bartleby.com/254/87.html [Accessed 13 May 2015].

Associated Press (2014) 'Game of Thrones' Brings Economic Boost to Northern Ireland. Available at http://www.hollywoodreporter.com/news/game-thrones-brings-economic-boost-714036. [Accessed 21 April 2015].

Ballve, M. (2013) 'Our List of the World's Largest Social Networks Shows How Video, Messages, And China Are Taking Over the Social Web'. Available at http://www.businessinsider.com/the-worlds-largest-social-networks-2013-12?IR=T [Accessed 15 March 2015].

Barber, N. (2013) 'Why are Zombies Still So Popular?' Available at http://www.bbc.com/culture/story/20131025-zombie-nation [Accessed 30 March 2015].

Baudrillard, J. (1995) *Simulacra and Simulation (The Body in Theory: Histories of Cultural Materialism)*. 17th edition. Ann Arbor, MI: The University of Michigan Press.

Bay Hotel (no date) 'The Bay Hotel Port Isaac Cornwall'. Available at http://www.bayhotelportisaac.co.uk/ [Accessed 21 April 2015].

Bell, A. (2009) '"Twilight" Series Spawns Religion: Edward Cullen Is Real'. Available at http://www.examiner.com/article/twilight-series-spawns-religion-edward-cullen-is-real-members-should-read-the-books-like-a-bible [Accessed 15 March 2015].

Blistein, J. (2014) 'The Smiths Offer Up This Charming Timeline: New Interactive Timeline Features Music, Band History and Career Milestones'. Available at http://www.rollingstone.com/music/news/the-smiths-offer-up-this-charming-timeline-20140304 [Accessed 13 April 2015].

Boorstin, D. (1962/1997) *The Image: A Guide to Pseudo-events in America*. London, UK: Vintage Books.

Brooker, W. (2007) 'A Sort of Homecoming: Fan Viewing and Symbolic Pilgrimage'. in J. Gray, C. Sandvoss, and C. L. Harrington (eds) *Fandom: Identities and Communities in a Mediated World*. New York & London: New York University Press.

Brooker, W. (2005) '"It is Love": The Lewis Carroll Society as Fan Community'. In *American Behavioral Scientist*, Vol. 48 (7), 859–880.

Brooker, W. (1999) *Teach Yourself Cultural Studies*. New York: McGraw-Hill.

Burlingame, R. (2015) 'The Walking Dead Delivers Highest-Rated Season Finale Ever With 15.8 Million Viewers'. Available at http://comicbook.com/2015/03/30/the-walking-dead-delivers-highest-rated-series-finale-ever-with-/ [Accessed 21 April 2015].

Busby, G. & Haines, C. (2013) 'Doc Martin and Film Tourism: The Creation of Destination Image'. In Tourism: Preliminary Communication, Vol. 61 (2), 105–120.

Busby, G., Huang, R. & Jarman, R. (2013) 'The Stein Effect: An Alternative Film-Induced Tourism Perspective'. In International Journal of Tourism Research, Vol. 15 (6), 570–582.

Busby, G. & Hambly, Z. (2000) 'Literary Tourism and the Daphne du Maurier Festival'. In Cornish Studies, Vol. 8, 197–210.

Bynum, R. (2015) 'Movie Fans Can Visit Film Sites in Georgia: "Forrest Gump" Park Bench, "Deliverance" River and "Hunger Games" House are Popular Sites to Visit'. Available at http://jacksonville.com/breaking-news/2015-01-01/story/movie-fans-can-visit-film-sites-georgia [Accessed 11 May 2015].

Caroline (no date) 'Marc Bolan's Rock Shrine – A Place of Modern-day Pilgrimage'. Available at http://flickeringlamps.com/2014/09/16/marc-bolans-rock-shrine-a-place-of-modern-day-pilgrimage/ [Accessed 21 April 2015].

Chilton, M. (2014) 'Game of Thrones Boosts Spanish Town's Economy'. Available at http://www.telegraph.co.uk/culture/tvandradio/game-of-thrones/11181710/Game-of-Thrones-boosts-Spanish-towns-economy.html [Accessed 21 April 2015].

Connell, J. (2005) 'What's the Story in Balamory: The Impacts of a Children's TV Programme on Small Tourism Enterprises on the Isle of Mull'. In Journal of Sustainable Tourism, Vol. 13 (3), 228–251.

Control (2007) Dir. A. Corbijn. 3 Dogs and a Pony.

Crawshaw, C. & Urry, J. (2000) 'Tourism and the Photographing Eye'. In J. Urry & C. Rojek (eds) Touring Cultures: Transformations of Travel and Theory. London, UK: Routledge, pp. 176–195.

Crowther, G. (2010) 'Virtually There in Boston' special commemoration supplement of Plath Profiles Interdisciplinary Journal Vol 3, Indiana University, Indiana.

Croy, W.G. (2010) 'Planning for Film Tourism: Active Destination Image Management'. In Tourism and Hospitality Planning & Development, Vol. 7 (1), 21–30.

Crupi, A. (2015) 'Game of Thrones Sets Another Ratings Record 6.95 million viewers turn out for Sunday night's episode'. Available at http://www.adweek.com/news/television/game-thrones-sets-another-ratings-record-157335 [Accessed 21 April 2015].

Daphne du Maurier. Available at http://www.jamaicainn.co.uk/daphne-du-maurier [Accessed 29 April 2015].

DavidCDM (2014) 'Cornwall Is Officially the Poorest Area in the UK'. Available at http://www.westbriton.co.uk/Cornwall-officially-poorest-area-UK/story-21062714-detail/story.html [Accessed 9 April 2015].

Dickinson, E. (no date) 'Charlotte Brontë's Grave'. Available at http://www.readbookonline.net/readOnLine/12422/ [Accessed 13 May 2015].

Discover Forks Washington (2015) 'Twilight' Available at http://forkswa.com/twilight/ [Accessed 15 March 2015].

Doc Martin House (no date). Available at http://www.docmartinhouse.co.uk/index.html [Accessed 21 April 2015].

Duffet, M. (2003) 'False Faith or False Comparison? A Critique of the Religious Interpretation of Elvis Fan Culture'. In *Popular Music and Society*, Vol. 26 (4), 513–522.
Dyer, R. (2004) *Heavenly Bodies: Film Stars and Society*. 2nd edition. London & New York: Routledge.
Fakeye, P.C. & Crompton, J.L. (1991) 'Image Differences Between Prospective, First-time, and Repeat Visitors to the Lower Rio Grande Valley'. In *Journal of Travel Research*, Vol. 30 (2), 10–16.
FAQs About Visiting Graceland. Available at http://www.graceland.com/visit/plan_your_visit/faq.aspx [Accessed 5 March 2015].
'Fern Cottage: Port Isaac, Cornwall' (no date). Available at http://www.docmartinhouse.co.uk/ [Accessed 24 April 2015].
Fitzgerald, M. (1999) 'Stoned Immaculate'. Available at http://mfitzgeraldspage.com/Four%20Essays/morrison.pdf [Accessed 21 April 2015].
Foley, M. & Lennon, J. (2010) *Dark Tourism: The Attraction of Death and Disaster*. London, UK: Cengage Learning.
'Fowey's du Maurier Festival Name Changed' (2012). Available at http://www.bbc.co.uk/news/uk-england-cornwall-20478287 [Accessed 29 April 2015].
Fry, R.W. (2014) 'Becoming a "True Blues Fan": Blues Tourism and Performances of the King Biscuit Blues Festival'. In *Tourist Studies*, Vol. 14 (1), 66–85.
Gallagher, N. (2003) *Live Forever: The Rise and Fall of Brit Pop*. Dir. J. Dower. BBC.
Gatenby, P. and Gill, C. (2011) *Manchester Musical History Tour*. Manchester, England: Empire Publications Limited.
Gledhill, R. (2014) 'Exclusive: New Figures Reveal Massive Decline in Religious Affiliation'. Available at http://www.christiantoday.com/article/exclusive.new.figures.reveal.massive.decline.in.religious.affiliation/41799.htm [Accessed 15 March 2015].
Godwin, W. (1809), Essay on Sepulchers: or, A Proposal for Erecting Some Memorial of the Illustrious Dead in all Ages on the Spot where their remains have been interred'. In M. Philip (ed.) *Political and Philosophical Writings of William Godwin* (7 vols, 1993), VI 6.
Goldhill, S. (2011) *Freud's Couch, Scott's Buttocks, Brontes Grave: Cultural Trails: Adventures in Travel*. Chicago & London: University of Chicago Press.
Graceland Live Cam. Available at http://www.graceland.com/connect/graceland-cam.aspx [Accessed 15 March 2015].
Harriet (2015) Personal Interview,18 March 2015.
Harvard Institute for Religion Research (no date). Available at http://www.hartfordinstitute.org [Accessed 10 May 2015].
Haworth Village (no date). Available at http://www.haworth-village.org.uk/brontes/places/top_withens.asp [Accessed 13 May 2015].
Heitmann, S. (2010) 'Film Tourism Planning and Development Questioning the Role of Stakeholders and Sustainability'. In *Tourism and Hospitality Planning & Development*, Vol. 7 (1), 31–46.
Herbert, D.T. (2001) 'Literary Places, Tourism and the Heritage Experience'. In *Annals of Tourism Research*, Vol. 28 (2), 312–333.
Herbert, D.T. (1996) 'Artistic and Literary Places in France as Tourist Attractions'. In *Tourism Management*, Vol. 17 (2), 77–85.
Hills, M. (2002) *Fan Cultures*. London & New York: Taylor & Francis Group.

Hutchinson, L. (2014) 'The Mysterious Death of Jim Morrison'. Available at http://performingsongwriter.com/mysterious-death-jim-morrison/ [Accessed 13 April 2015].

Internet Live Stats (2014) 'Internet Live Stats'. Available at http://www.internet livestats.com/ [Accessed 15 March 2015].

Internet Live Stats (2015) 'Internet Live Stats'. Available at http://www.internet livestats.com/ [Accessed 15 March 2015].

Internet Resources to Accompany the Sourcebook for Teaching Science (no date). Available from http://www.csun.edu/science/health/docs/tv&health.html [Accessed 27 March 2015].

Iwashita, C. (2008) 'Roles of Films and Television Dramas in International Tourism: The Case of Japanese Tourists to the UK'. In *Journal of Travel & Tourism Marketing*, Vol. 24 (2–3), 139–151.

Jenkins, H. (1992) *Textual Poachers: Television Fans and Participatory Culture* (Studies in Culture and Communication). London & New York: Routledge.

Joy Division (2007) Dir. Grant Gee. Brown Owl Films.

Karaian, J. (2015) 'Game of Thrones Tourism Supports Europes Weakest Economies'. Available at https://www.toovia.com/posts/2015/apr/03/0.13503.6103713751 55118090 [Accessed 21 April 2015].

Kaul, A. (2014) 'Music on the Edge: Busking at the Cliffs of Moher and the Commodification of a Musical Landscape'. In *Tourism Studies*, Vol. 14 (1), 30–47.

Kim, S. (2011) 'Audience Involvement and Film Tourism Experiences: Emotional Places, Emotional Experiences'. In *Tourism Management*, Vol. 33 (2), 387–396.

Kinney, D. (2014) *The Dylanologists: Adventures in the Land of Bob*. New York: Simon & Schuster.

Kirshenblatt-Gimblett, B. (1995) 'Theorizing Heritage'. In *Ethnomusicology*, Vol. 39 (3), 367–380.

Kray, R.W. (2014) 'Becoming a "True Blues Fan": Blues Tourism and Performances of the King Biscuit Blues Festival'. In *Tourist Studies*, Vol. 14 (1), 66–85.

Lawson, M. (2013) 'Are We Really in a "Second Golden Age for Television"?' Available at http://www.theguardian.com/tv-and-radio/tvandradioblog/2013/may/23/second-golden-age-television-soderbergh [Accessed 21 April 2015].

Light, D. (2007) 'Dracula Tourism in Romania: Cultural Identity and the State'. *Annals of Tourism Research*, 34 (3), 746–765.

Live Forever: The Rise and Fall of Brit Pop (2003) Dir. J. Dower. BBC.

Long, P. (2014) 'Popular Music, Psychogeography, Place Identity and Tourism: The Case of Sheffield'. In *Tourism Studies*, Vol. 14 (1), 48–65.

Macaskill, H. (2013) 'The Road to Manderley: Exploring the Cornwall That Inspired Daphne du Maurier'. Available at http://www.dailymail.co.uk/travel/article-2315840/Exploring-Cornish-corners-inspired-Daphne-du-Mauriers-Rebecca.html [Accessed 29 April 2015].

MacPhail, B. (no date) 'Deliver Us From Salad Bar Religion'. Available at http://www.reformedtheology.ca/revelation2b.htm [Accessed 15 March 2015].

Mallinder, S. (2011) 'Movement: Journey of the Beat'. Unpublished PhD thesis, School of Media Communication and Culture, Murdoch University, Murdoch, WA, Australia.

Margry, P.J. (2007) 'The Performance of a Cult of the Sense: A Feast of Fans at Jim Morrison's Grave in Paris'. In *Traditiones*, Vol. 36/1, 141–152.

Marshall, P.D. (1997) *Celebrity and Power: Fame in Contemporary Culture*. Minneapolis, MN: University of Minnesota Press.

Marx, K. (1843) *Marx's Critique of Hegel's Philosophy of Right*. A. Jolin and J. O'Malley (trans.); J. O'Malley (ed.); A. Blunden (transcribed). Cambridge: Cambridge University Press, 1970. Available at https://www.marxists.org/archive/marx/works/1843/critique-hpr/ [Accessed 27 March 2015].

McSwain, S. (2014) 'Why Nobody Wants to Go to Church Anymore'. Available at http://www.huffingtonpost.com/steve-mcswain/why-nobody-wants-to-go-to_b_4086016.html [Accessed 15 March 2015].

Merchants of Cool (2001) [DVD] Dir. B. Goodman. Frontline.

Miller, J. (2014) 'Britons Spend More Time on Tech Than Asleep, Study Suggests'. Available at http://www.bbc.co.uk/news/technology-28677674 [Accessed 15 March 2015].

MozArmy (no date). Available at https://www.facebook.com/pages/Mozarmy/120886587984785 [Accessed 13 May 2015].

MozArmy Meet-up (no date). Available at http://www.morrissey-solo.com/content/1272-Mozarmy-meetup-May-25th-26th-2013-Manchester [Accessed 13 May 2015].

NME (2013) 'The Smiths' "The Queen Is Dead" Tops NME's List of 500 Greatest Albums of All Time'. Available at http://www.nme.com/news/the-smiths/73363#qERZ1e0y1TWvyJZE.99 [Accessed 21 April 2015].

Neely, C. (2013) '"The Walking Dead" Spreads New Life'. Available at http://www.times-herald.com/business/20130811-WalkingDeadFeature [Accessed 21 April 2015].

Nunes, M. (2001) 'Ephemeral Cities: Postmodern Urbanism and the Production of Online Space'. In Holmes, D. (ed.) *Virtual Globalization: Virtual Spaces/Tourist Spaces*. London & New York: Routledge.

Ofcom (2014) 'Adults' Media Use and Attitudes Report 2014'. Available at http://stakeholders.ofcom.org.uk/market-data-research/other/research-publications/adults/adults-media-lit-14/ [Accessed 15 March 2015].

Office for National Statistics (2013) 'Statistical Bulletin: Internet Access – Households and Individuals, 2013'. Available at http://www.ons.gov.uk/ons/rel/rdit2/internet-access---households-and-individuals/2013/stb-ia-2013.html [Accessed 15 March 2015].

Petronzio, M. (2014) 'U.S. Adults Spend 11 Hours Per Day With Digital Media'. Available at http://mashable.com/2014/03/05/american-digital-media-hours/ [Accessed 15 March 2015].

Plate, L. (2006) 'Walking in Virginia Woolf's Footsteps: Performing Cultural Memory'. In *European Journal of Cultural Studies*, Vol. 9 (1), 101–120.

Port Isaac & Portwenn: Walk & Talk Guided Tours (no date). Available at http://www.portisaactours.com/ [Accessed 21 April 2015].

Putnam, R.D. (2001) *Bowling Alone: The Collapse and Revival of American Community*. New York: Touchstone Books, Simon & Schuster.

Rainer, T. (2013) '13 Issues for Churches in 2013'. Available at http://www.churchleaders.com/pastors/pastor-articles/164787-thom-rainer-13-issues-churches-2013.html [Accessed 24 April 2015].

Reijnders, S. (2011) 'Stalking the Count: Dracula, Fandom and Tourism'. In *Annals of Tourism Research*, Vol. 38 (1), 231–248.

Richardson, M. (2001) 'The Gift of Presence: The Act of Leaving Artifacts at Shrines, Memorials and Other Tragedies'. In Adams, O., Hoelscher, S. & Till, K. (eds) *Textures of Place: Exploring Humanist Geographies*. Minneapolis, MN: University of Minnesota Press, pp. 257–272.

Riley, R.W. (1994) 'Movie-induced Tourism'. In Seato, A.V. (ed.) *Tourism: State of the Art*. Chichester, England: John Wiley & Sons, p. 453–458.

Roberts, L. (2014) 'Marketing Music Scales, or the Political Economy of Contagious Music'. In *Tourist Studies*, Vol. 14 (1), 10–29.

Rodman, G.B. (1996) *Elvis After Elvis: The Posthumous Career of a Living Legend*. London: Routledge.

Rojek, C. (2001) *Celebrity*. London: Reaktion Books.

Rojek, C. (1997) 'Indexing, Dragging and the Social Construction of Tourist Sights'. In Rojek, C. & Urry, J. (eds) *Touring Cultures, Transformations of Travel and Theory*. London: Routledge, pp. 52–73.

Rojek, C. (1993) *Ways of Escape: Modern Transformations in Leisure and Travel*. London: Palgrave Macmillan.

Rolfe, P. (2014) '"Game of Thrones" Shoot Boosts Tourism 15 Percent in Spain's Seville'. Available at http://www.hollywoodreporter.com/news/gamepthrones-boosts-spain-tourism-745017 [Accessed 21 April 2015].

Roue, L. (2015) 'The Smiths, Oasis and Happy Mondays – the Man Helping You Follow in the Footsteps of Your Favorite Manchester Bands'. Available at http://www.manchestereveningnews.co.uk/business/smiths-oasis-happy-mondays---8542826 [Accessed 14 April 2015].

Run for Your Lives (no date). Available at http://runforyourlives.com.au/; https://www.youtube.com/watch?v=eKEVbC0GiUg [Accessed 13 May 2015].

Sandvoss, C. (2005) *Fans: The Mirror of Consumption*. Malden, MA: Polity Press.

Shadowplayers: The Rise and Fall of Factory Records (2006) Dir. J. Nice. LTM Recordings.

Simon, P. (1986) *Graceland*, Warner Brothers.

Soliman, M.D. (2011) 'Exploring the Role of Film in Promoting Domestic Tourism: A Case Study of Al Fayoum, Egypt, In *Journal of Vacation Marketing*, Vol. 17 (3), 225–235.

Squire, S.J. (1996a) 'Landscapes, Places and Geographic Spaces: Texts of Beatrix Potter as Cultural Communication'. In *GeoJournal*, Vol. 38 (1), 75–86.

Squire, S.J. (1996b) 'Literary Tourism and Sustainable Tourism: Promoting "Anne of Green Gables" in Prince Edward Island'. In *Journal of Sustainable Tourism*, Vol. 4 (3), 119–134.

Squire, S.J. (1994) 'The Cultural Values of Literary Tourism'. In *Annals of Tourism Research*, Vol. 21 (1), 104.

Stoker, B. (1897) *Dracula*. Available at http://www.pagebypagebooks.com/Bram_Stoker/Dracula/CHAPTER_8_p2.html [Accessed 24 April 2015].

Tabrys, J. (2014) '"The Walking Dead" Planned Through to Season 12'. Available at http://screenrant.com/walking-dead-plot-season-12/ [Accessed 30 March 15].

TAG's Free Access Marc Bolan and T. Rex Site. Available at http://Marc-Bolan.org [Accessed 24 April 2015].

Tetley, S. (1998) 'Visitor Attitudes to Authenticity at a Literary Destination'. PhD thesis, Sheffield Hallam University, England.

The Harry Potter Alliance (2005) Available at http://www.thehpalliance.org [Accessed 15 March 2015].

The Official Marc Bolan (TOMB). Available at http://www.tilldawn.net/tomb.html [Accessed 21 April 2015].

The Official Marc Bolan Fan Club. Available at http://www.marc-bolan.com/ [Accessed 24 April 2015].

Traub, C. (no date) 'Top 10 Paris Tourist Attractions and Unforgettable Sights'. Available at http://goparis.about.com/od/sightsattractions/tp/ParisTopTen.htm [Accessed 21 April 2015].

Trip Advisor (no date a) 'Walking Dead Tour'. Available at http://www.tripadvisor. co.uk/ShowUserReviews-g60898-d2646993-r140946837-Atlanta_Movie_Tours-Atlanta_Georgia.html [Accessed 24 April 2015].

Trip Advisor (no date b) 'Doc Martin Has Left the Village!' Available at http://www. tripadvisor.co.uk/ShowUserReviews-g186242-r85068039-Port_Isaac_Cornwall_ England.html [Accessed 21 April 2015].

Tzanelli, R. (2003) 'Casting the Neohellenic "Other": Tourism, the Culture Industry, and Contemporary Orientalism in "Captain Corelli's Mandolin". In *Journal of Consumer Culture*, Vol. 3 (2), 217–244.

Urry, J. (1990) *The Tourist Gaze.* London, UK: Sage Publications.

Visit Cornwall (no date). Available at https://www.visitcornwall.com/places/port-isaac#.VSZQbxcOwfo [Accessed 21 April 2015].

Walking Dead Locations. Available at http://walkingdeadlocations.com [Accessed 24 April 2015].

Watson, N.J. (2006) *The Literary Tourist: Readers and Places in Romantic and Victorian Britain.* Basingstoke: Palgrave Macmillan.

Wilson, T. (2007) *Joy Division.* Dir. Grant Gee. Brown Owl Films.

Woolf, V. (1980 [1904]) 'Haworth, November 1904'. In Barrett, M. (ed.) *V. Woolf, Women and Writing.* New York: Harcourt Brace Jovanovich, pp. 121–125.

INDEX